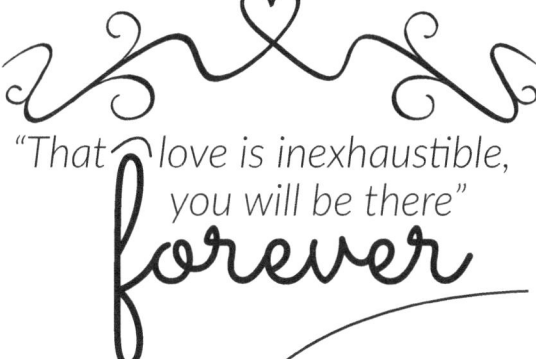

"That love is inexhaustible,
you will be there"
forever

_____

_____

_____

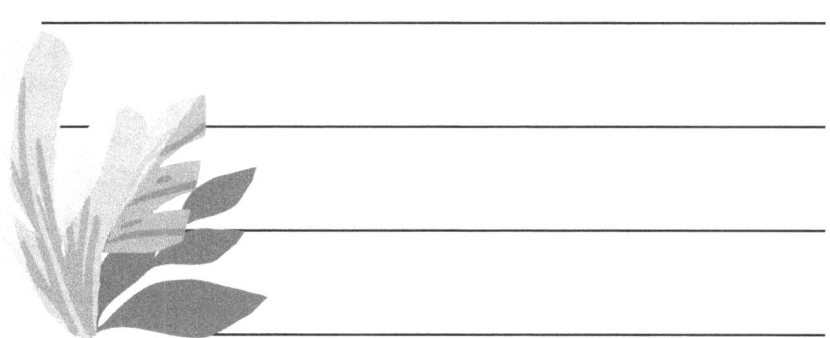

_____

_____

THIS BOOK
Belongs to

_____

Anatomy Coloring Book

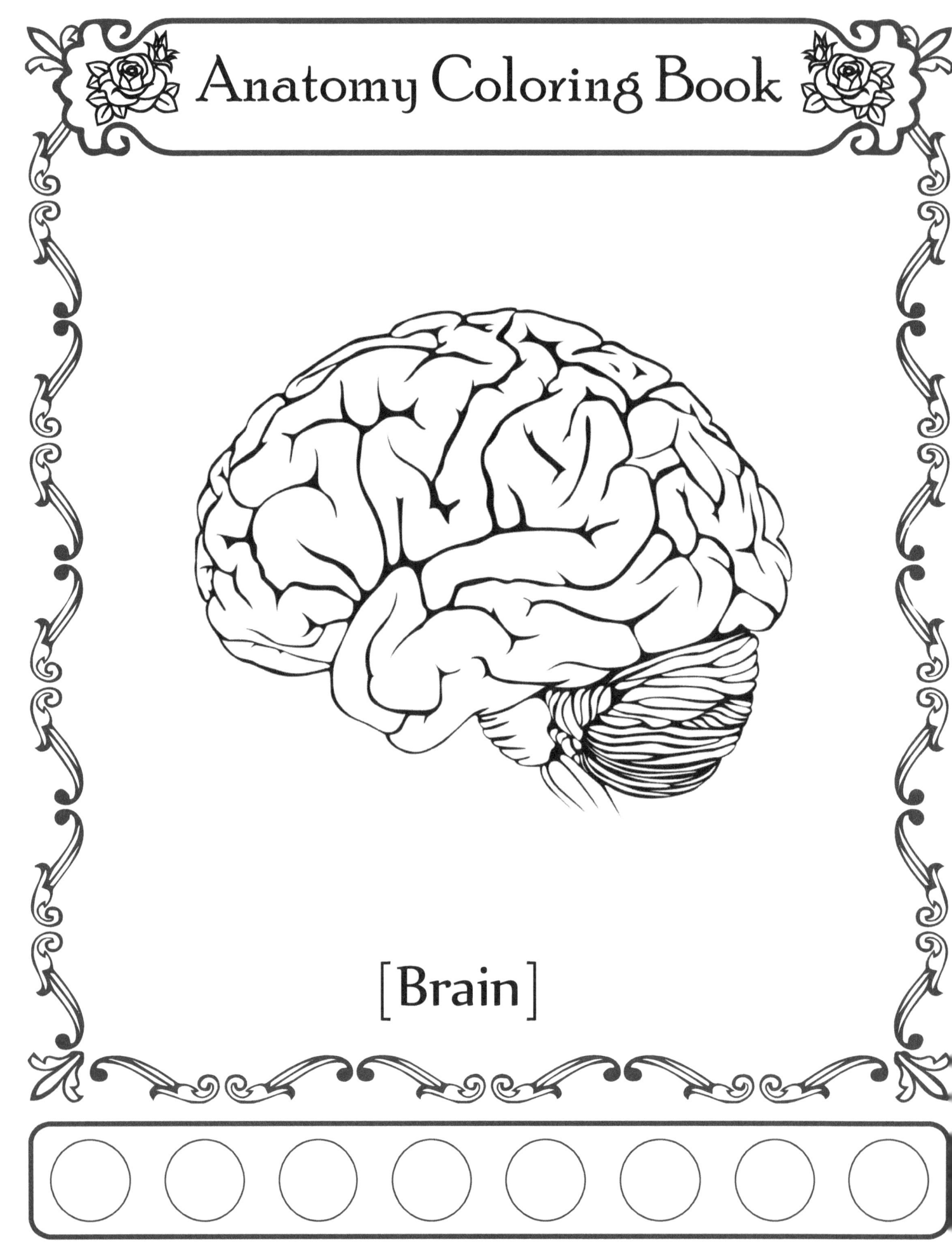

[Brain]

Anatomy Coloring Book

Anatomy Coloring Book

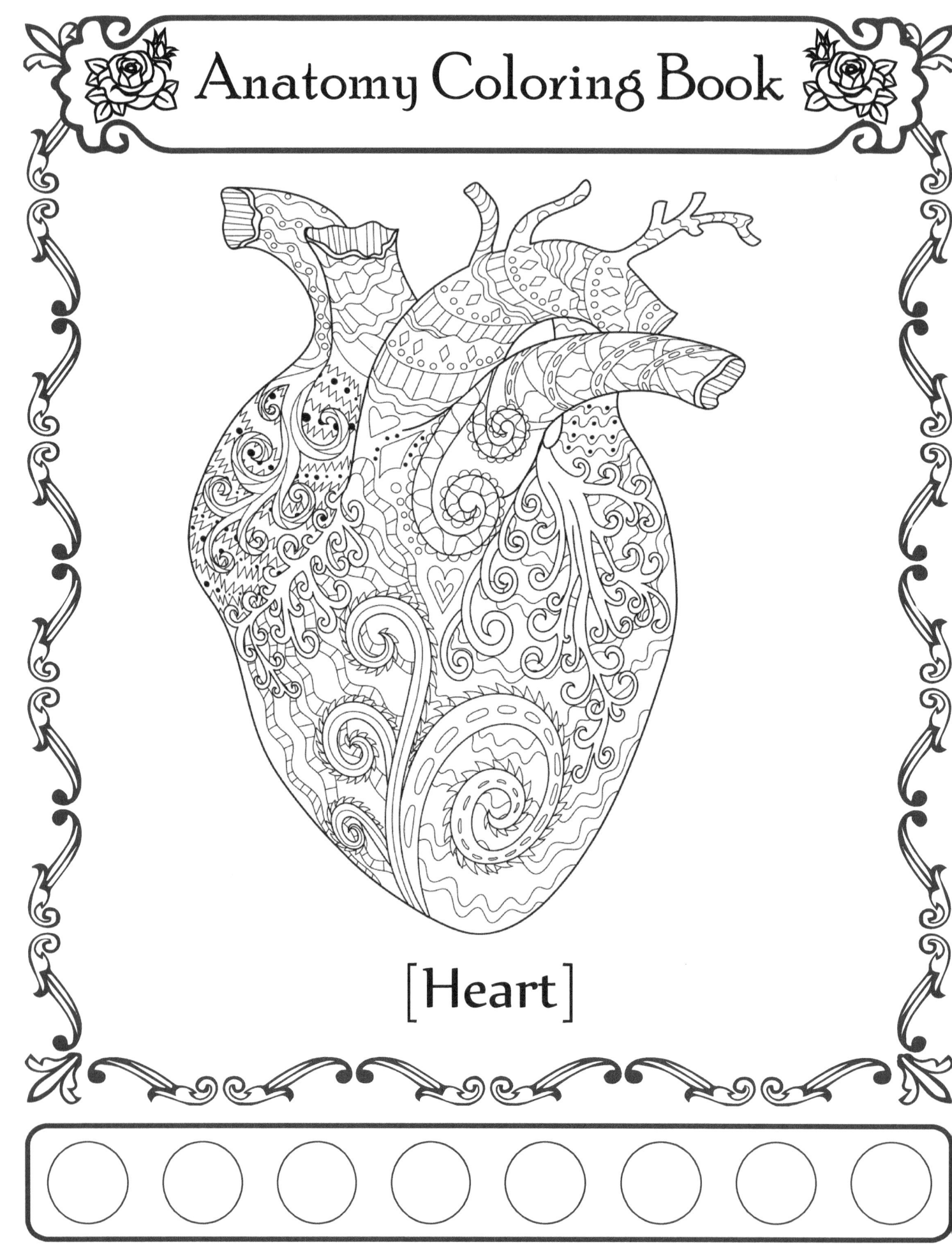

[Heart]

Anatomy Coloring Book

Anatomy Coloring Book

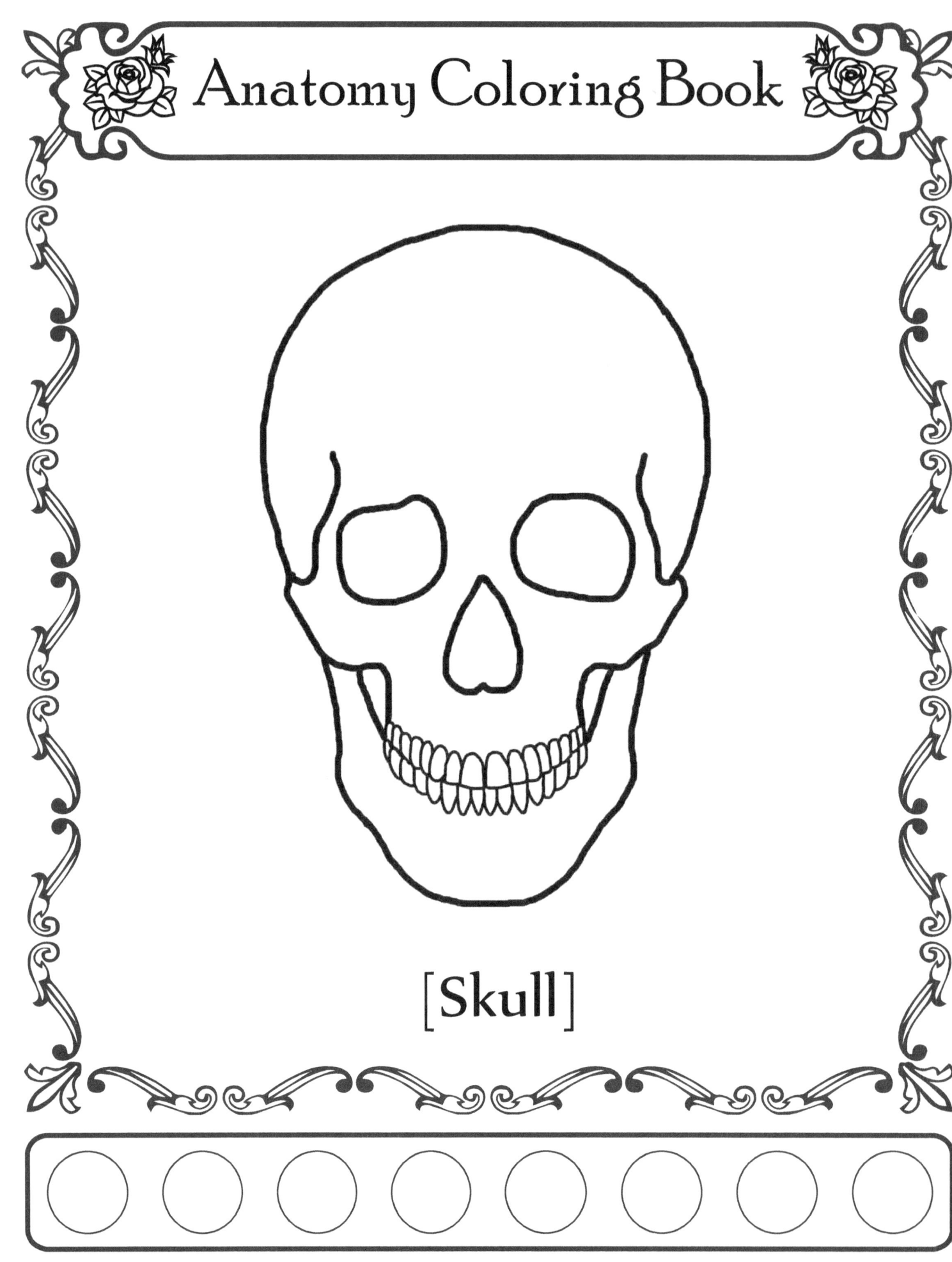

[Skull]

Anatomy Coloring Book

Anatomy Coloring Book

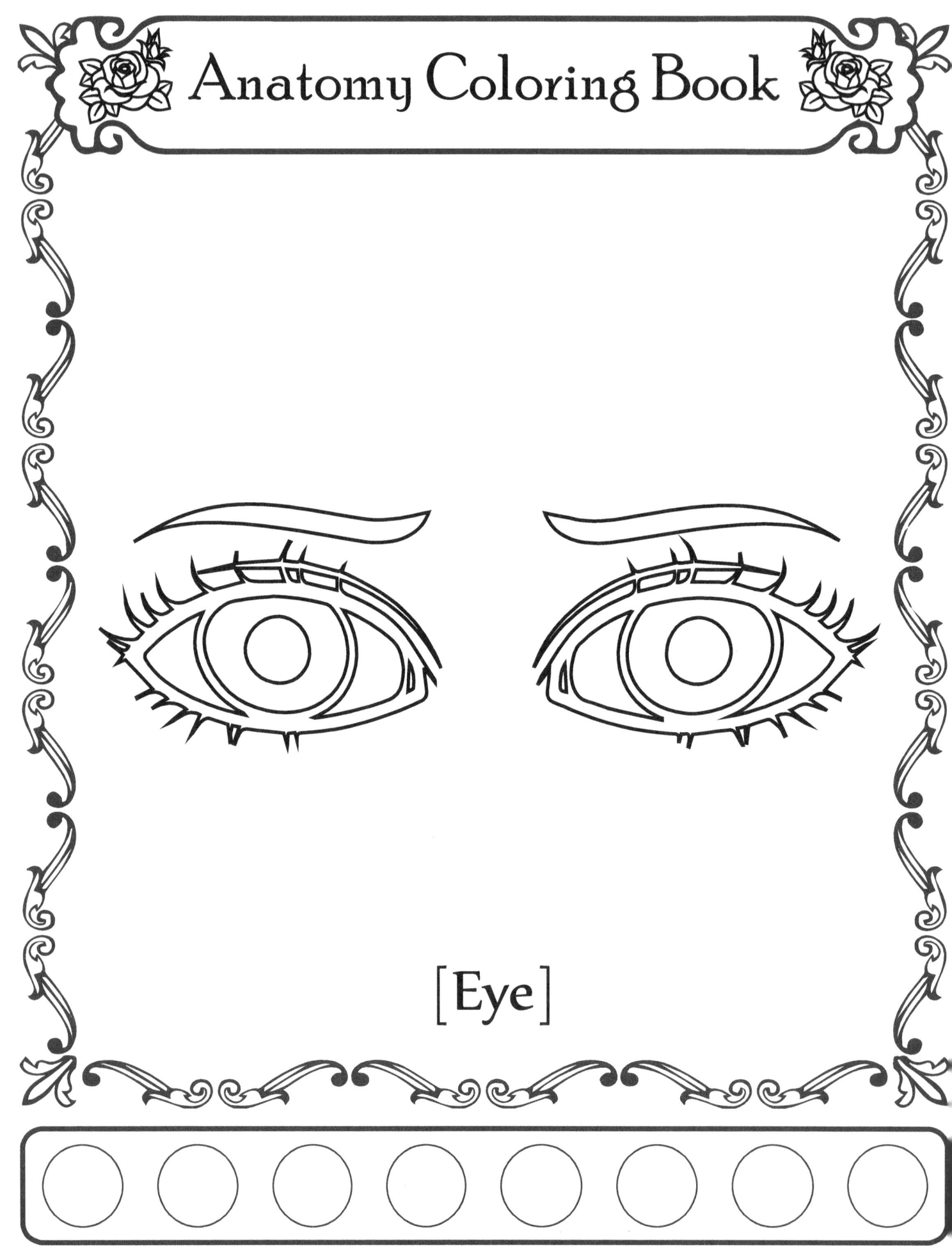

[Eye]

Anatomy Coloring Book

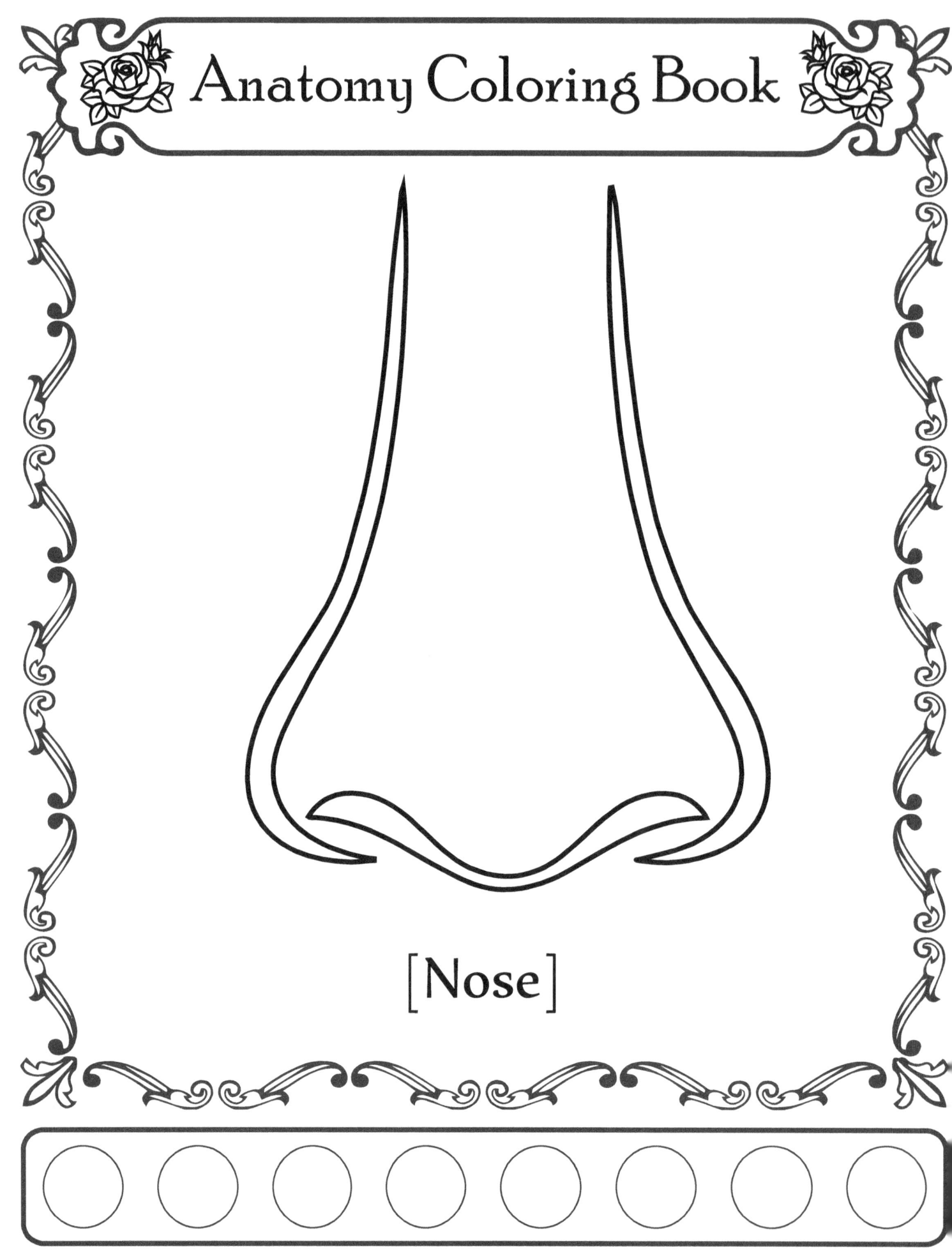

Anatomy Coloring Book

[Nose]

Anatomy Coloring Book

Anatomy Coloring Book

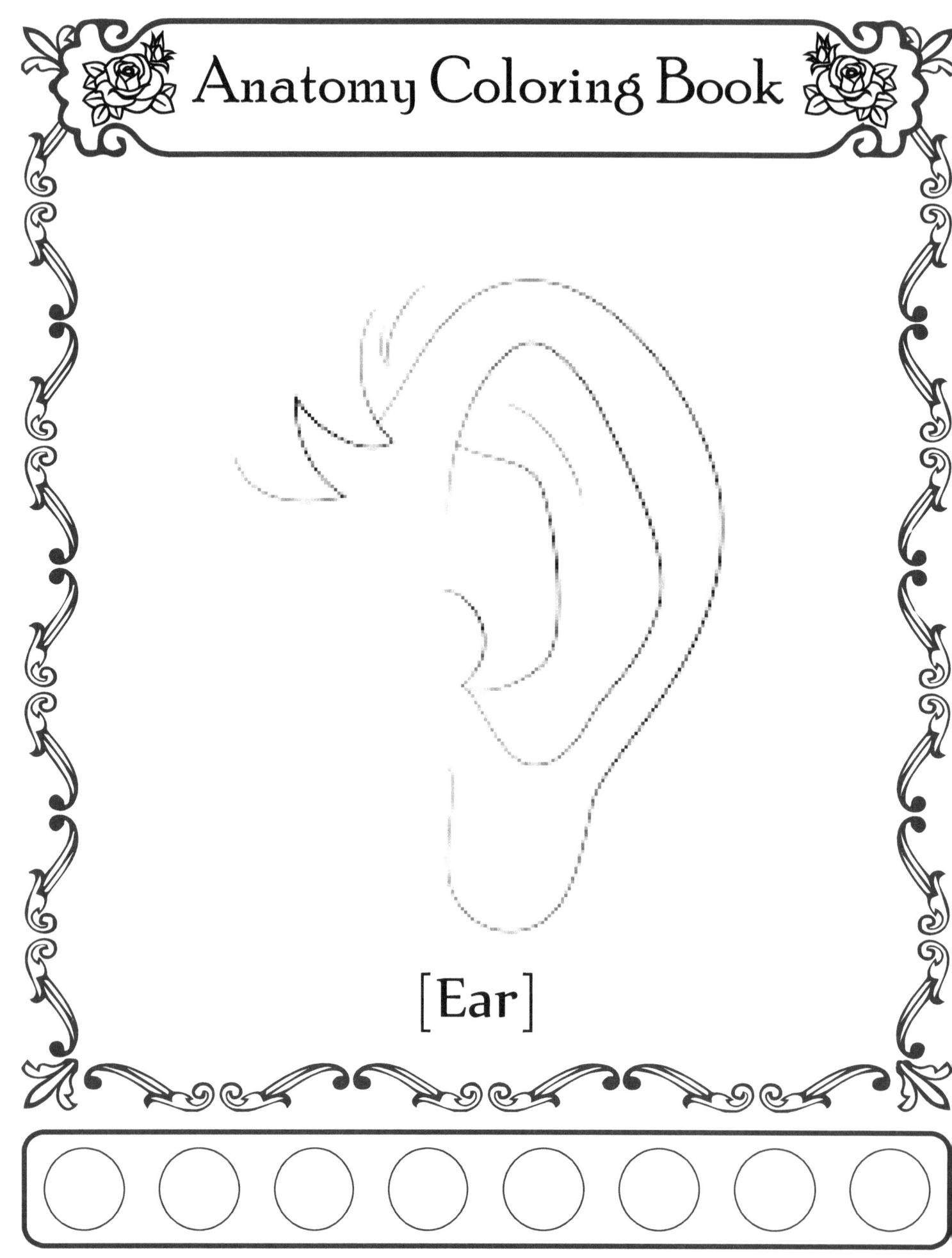

[Ear]

Anatomy Coloring Book

Anatomy Coloring Book

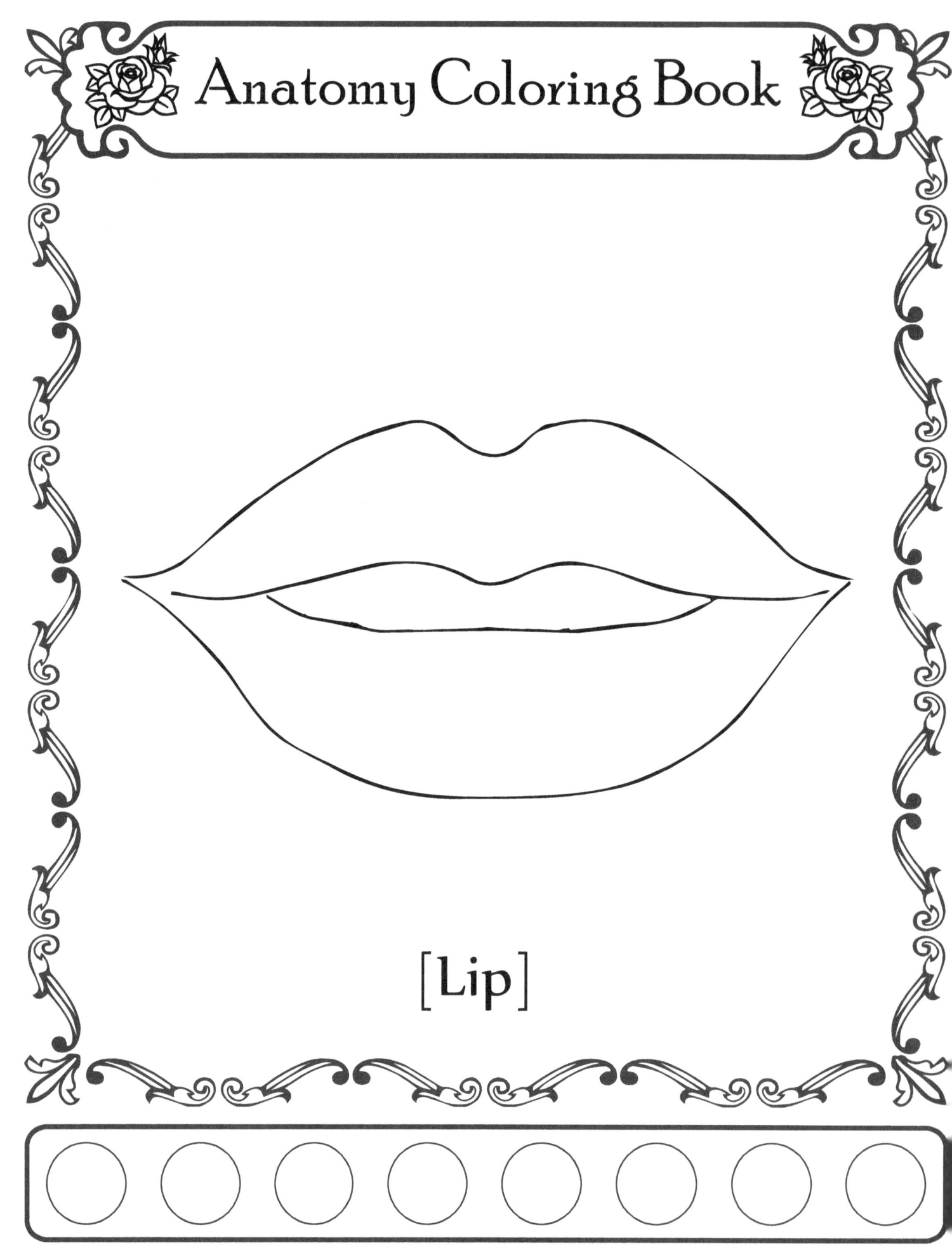

[Lip]

Anatomy Coloring Book

Anatomy Coloring Book

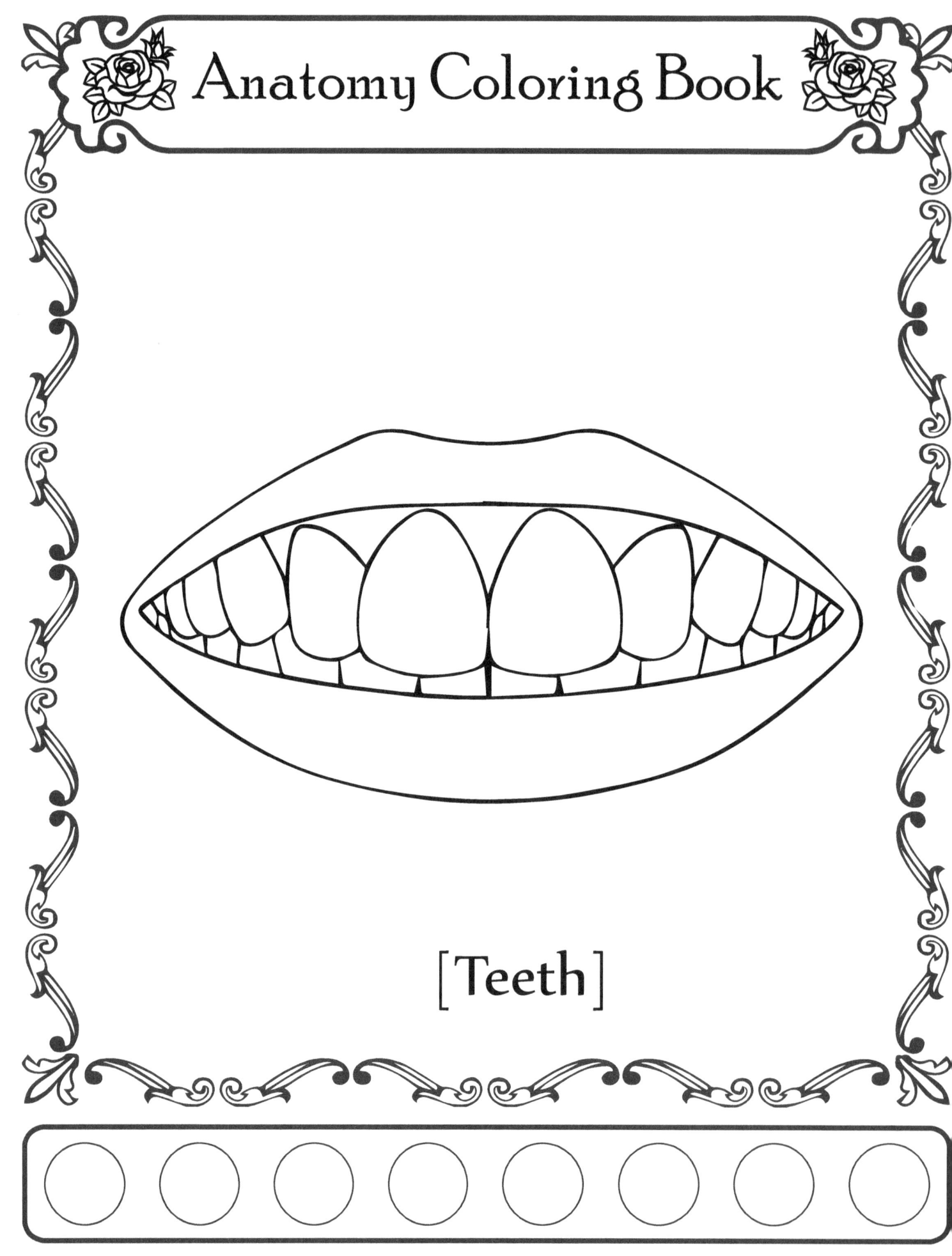

[Teeth]

Anatomy Coloring Book

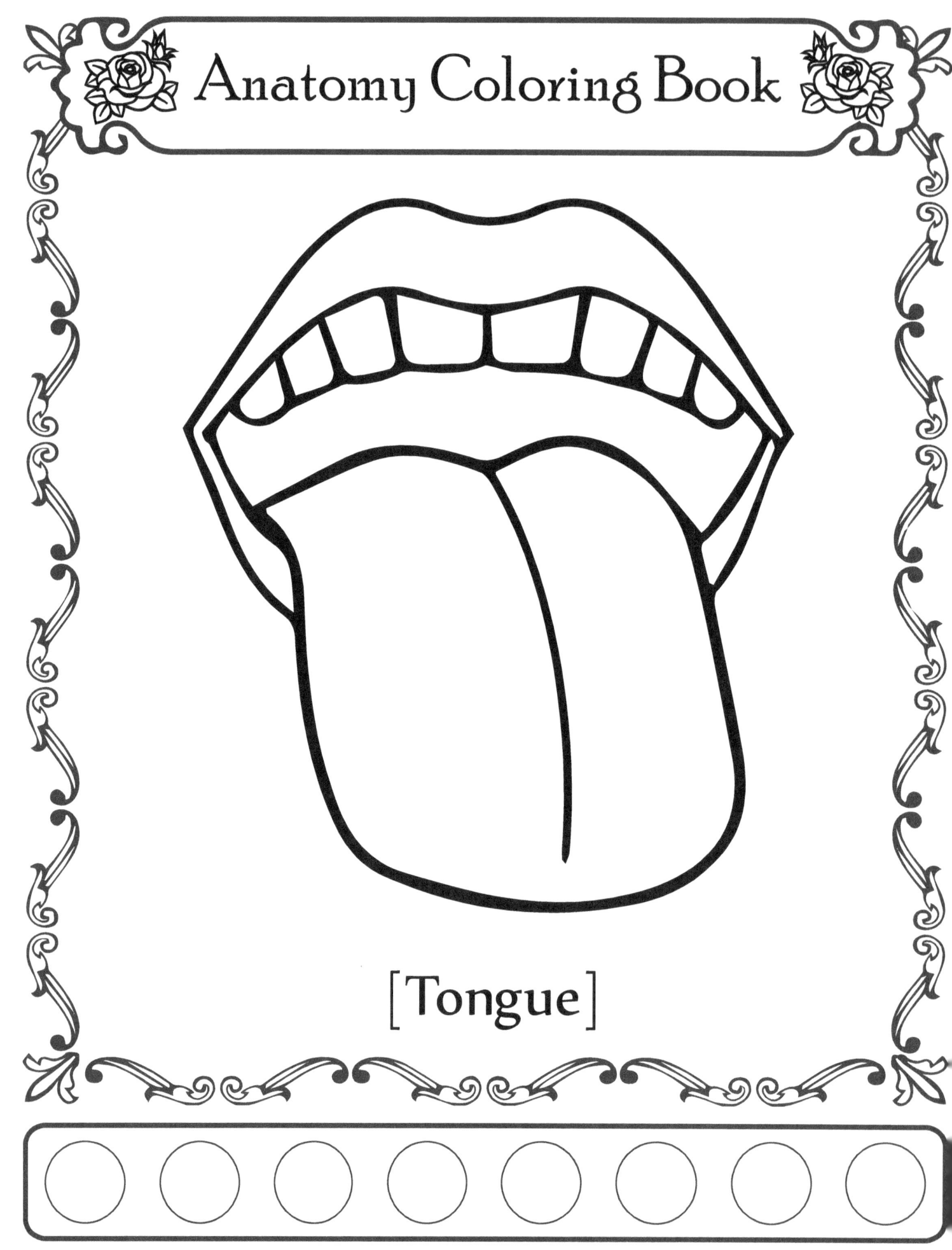

Anatomy Coloring Book

[Tongue]

Anatomy Coloring Book

Anatomy Coloring Book

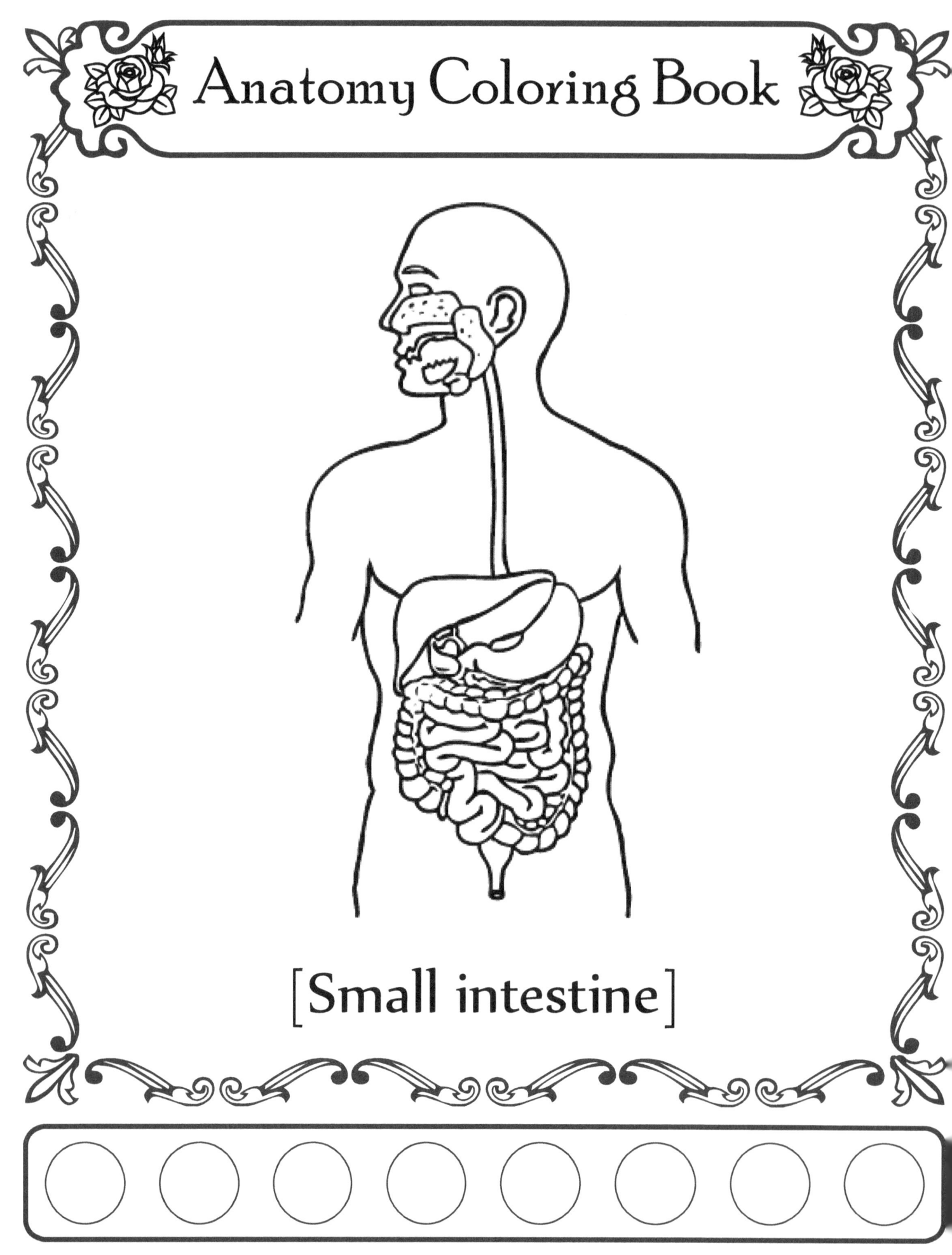

[Small intestine]

Anatomy Coloring Book

Anatomy Coloring Book

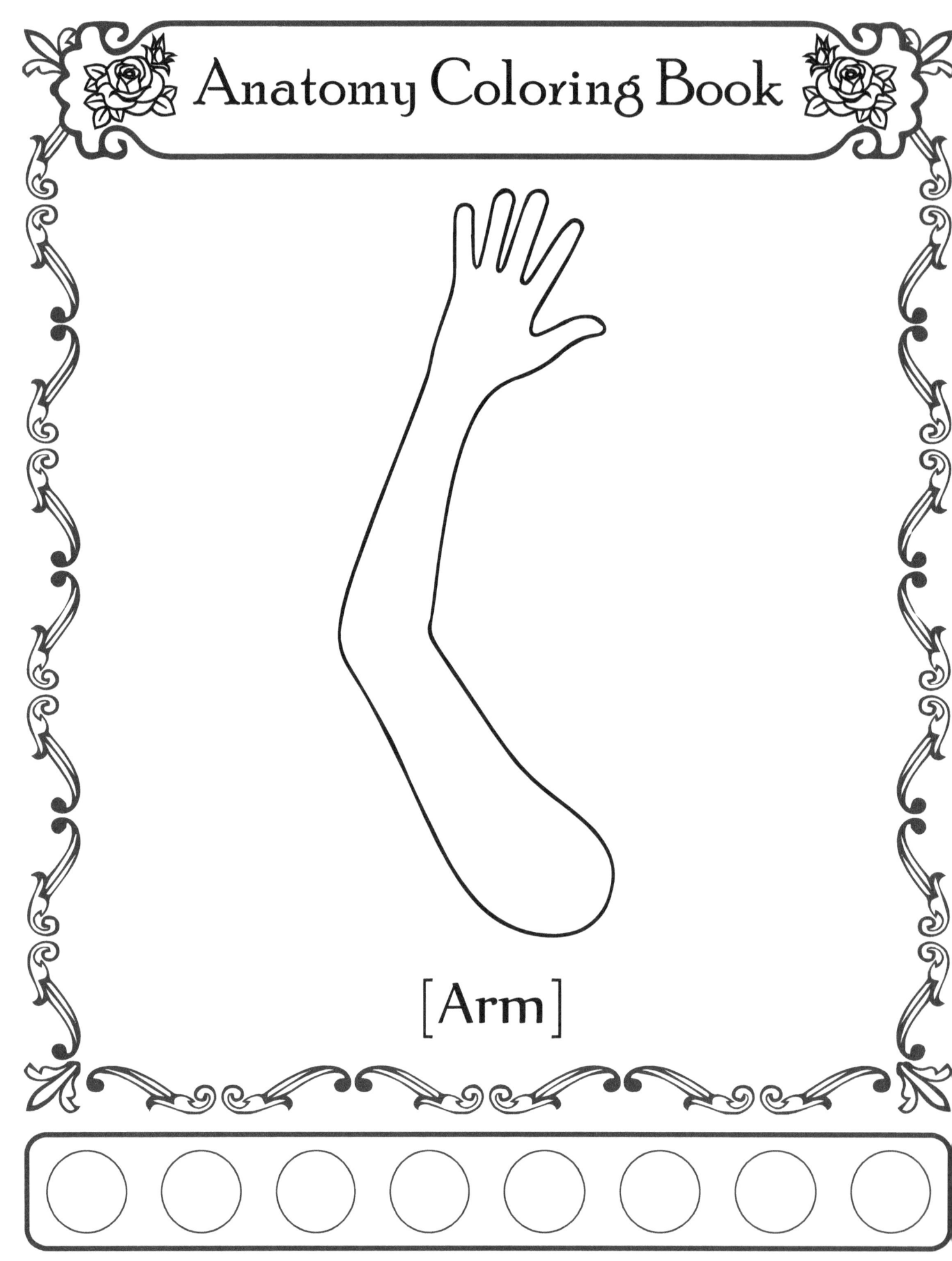

[Arm]

Anatomy Coloring Book

Anatomy Coloring Book

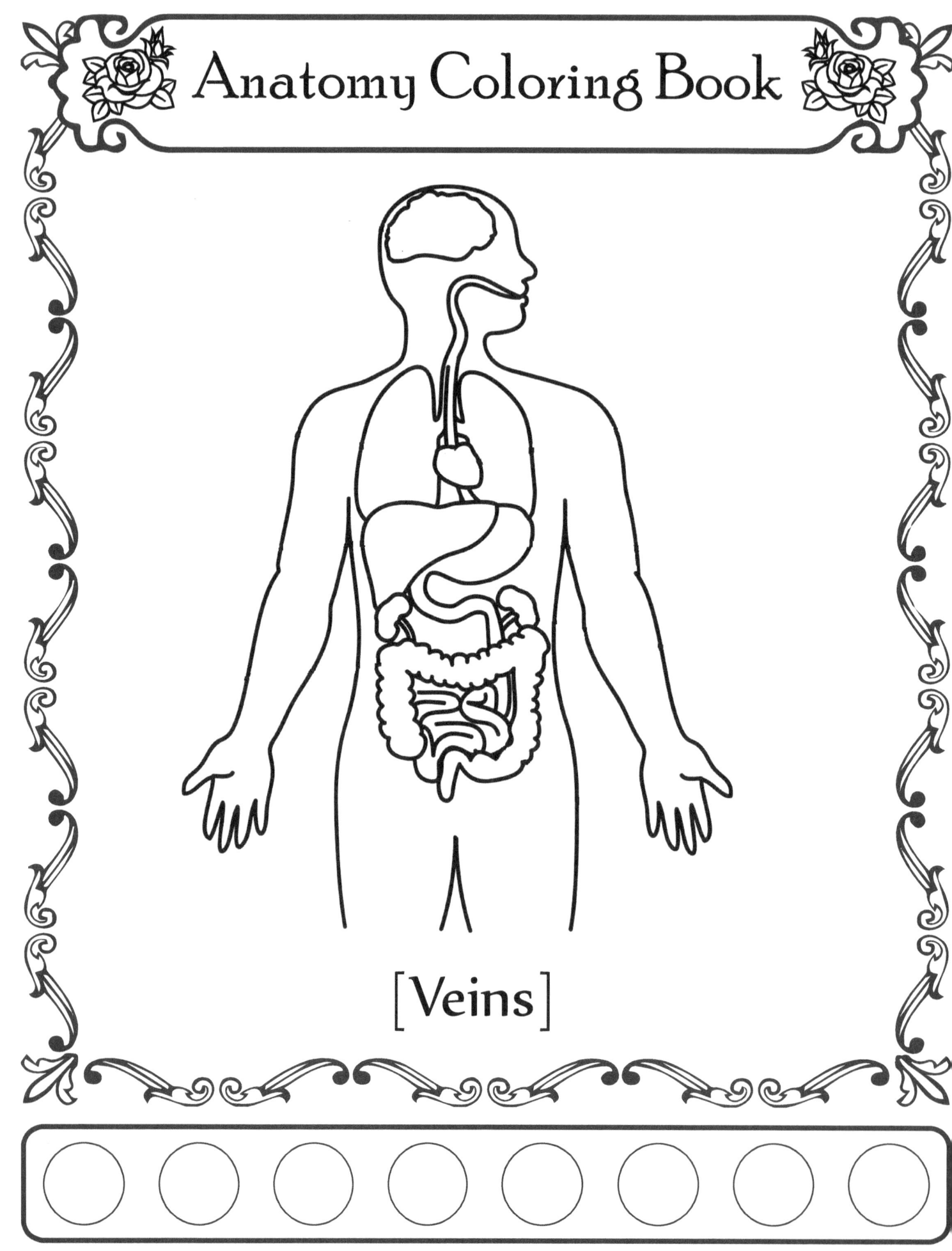

[Veins]

Anatomy Coloring Book

Anatomy Coloring Book

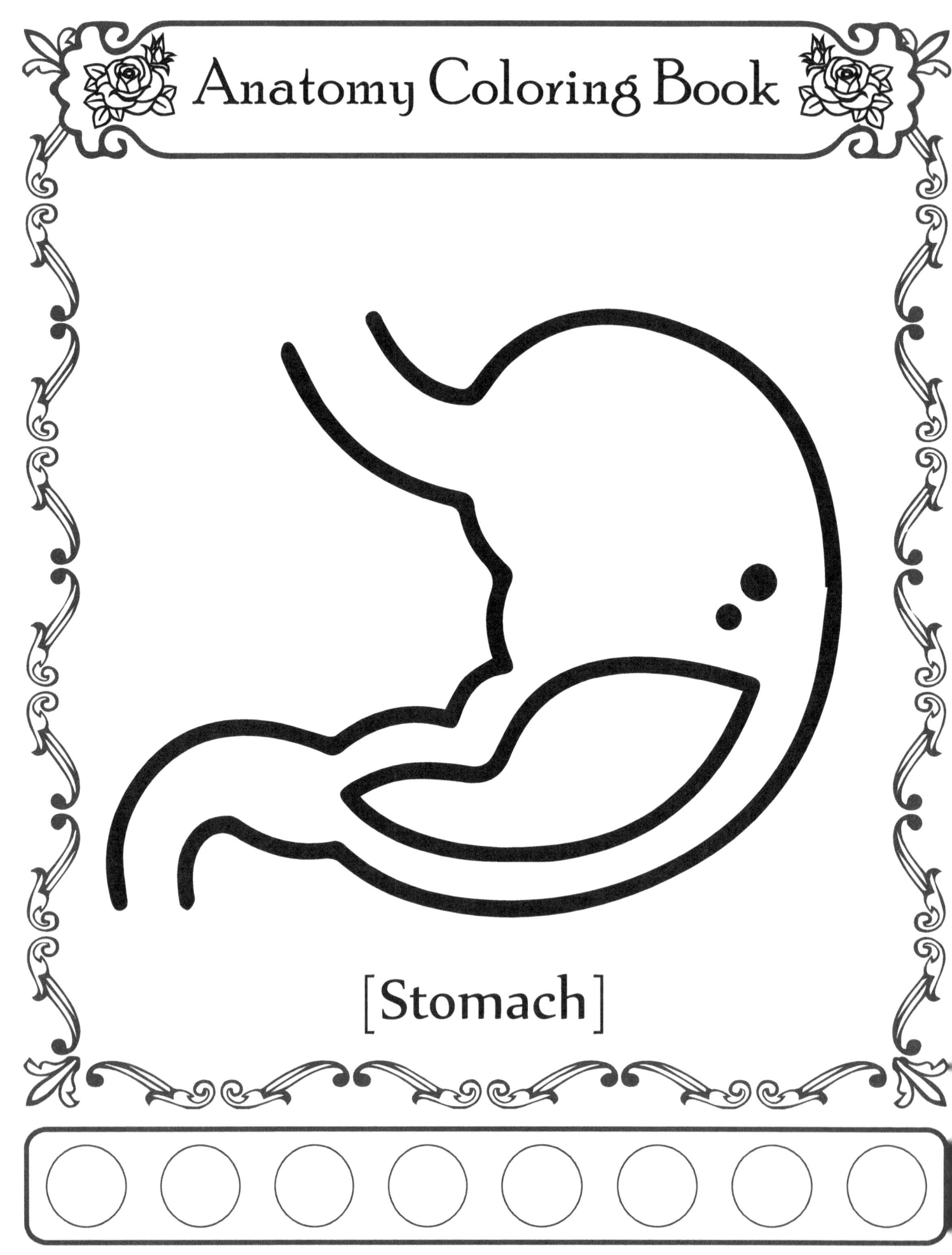

[Stomach]

Anatomy Coloring Book

Anatomy Coloring Book

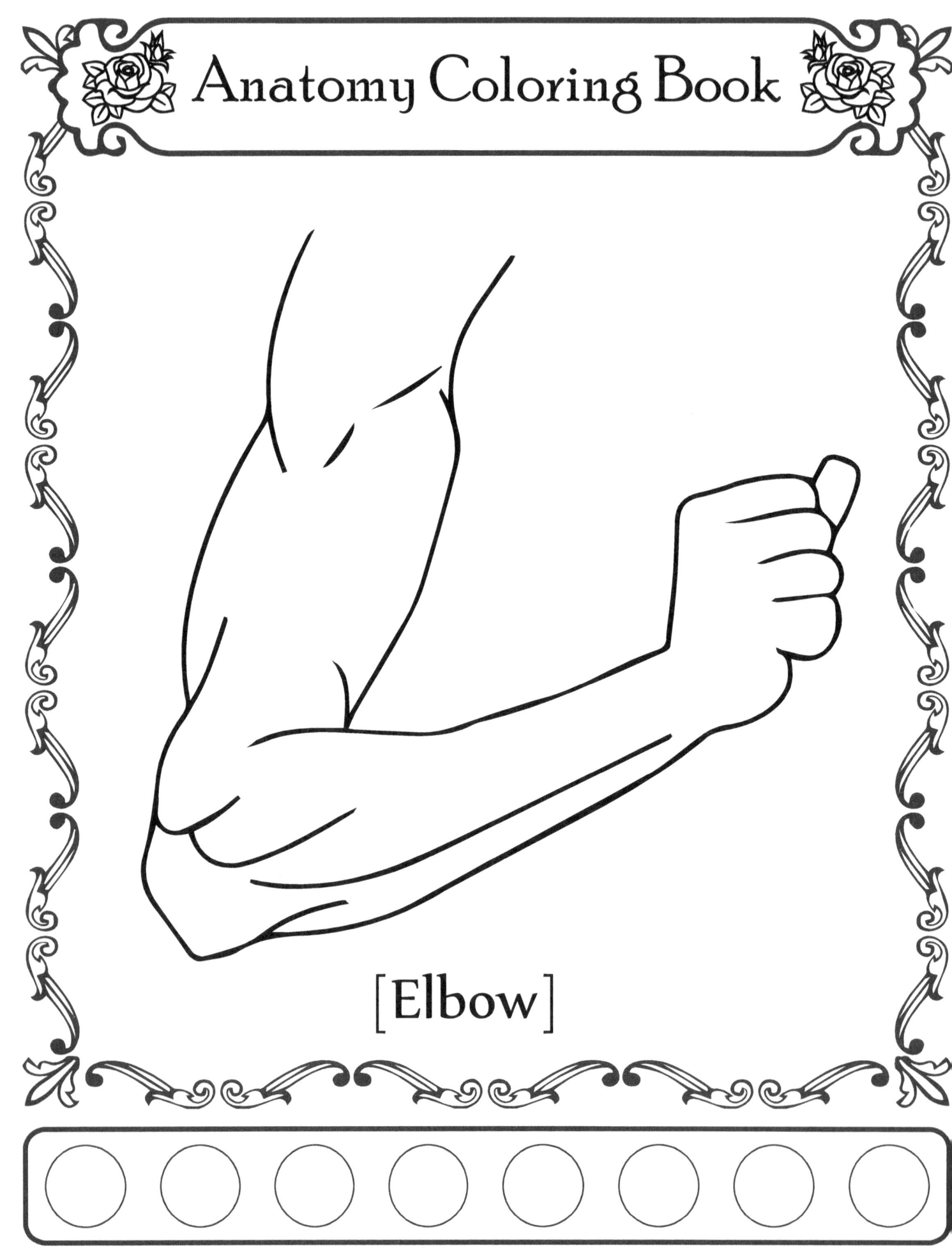

[Elbow]

Anatomy Coloring Book

Anatomy Coloring Book

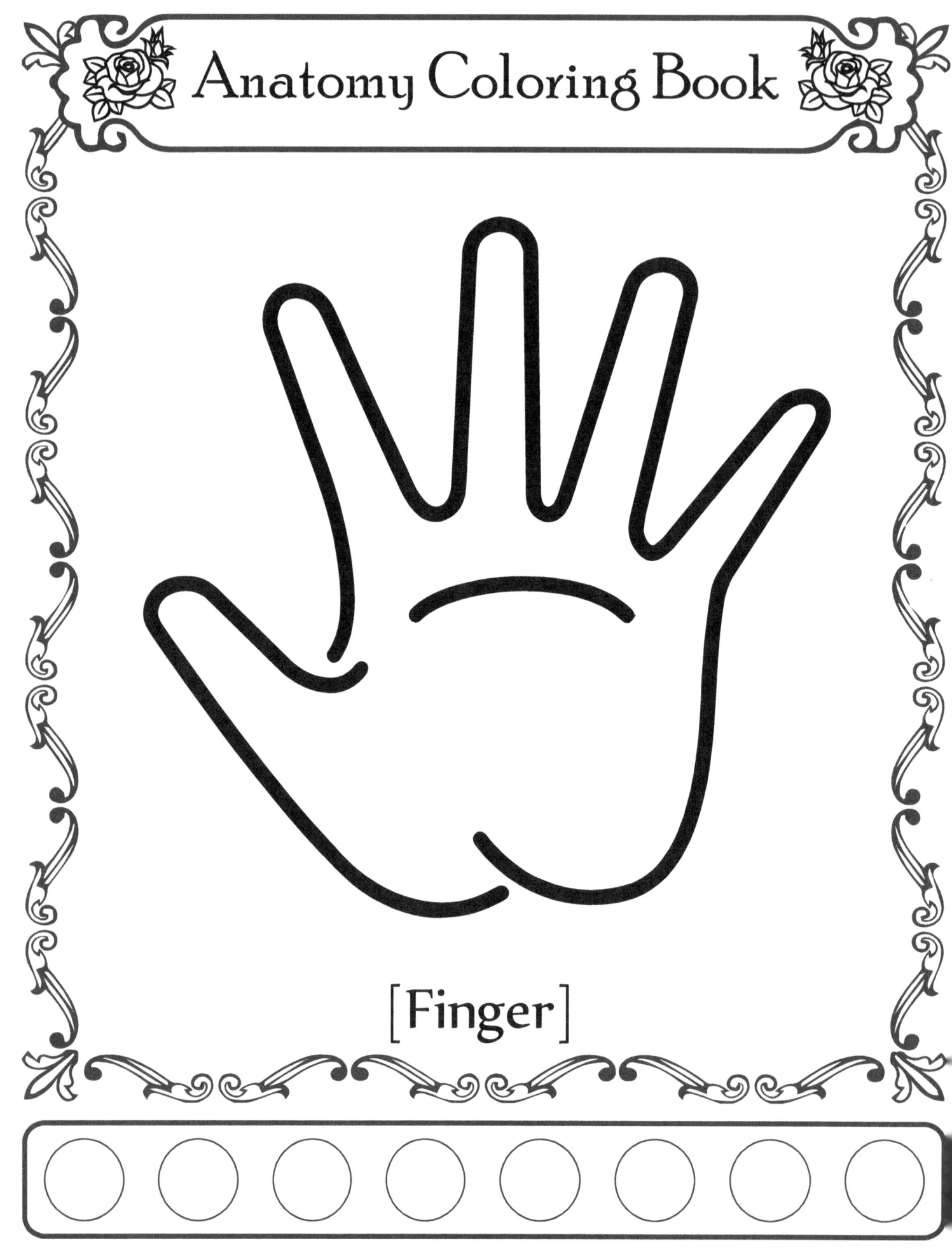

[Finger]

Anatomy Coloring Book

Anatomy Coloring Book

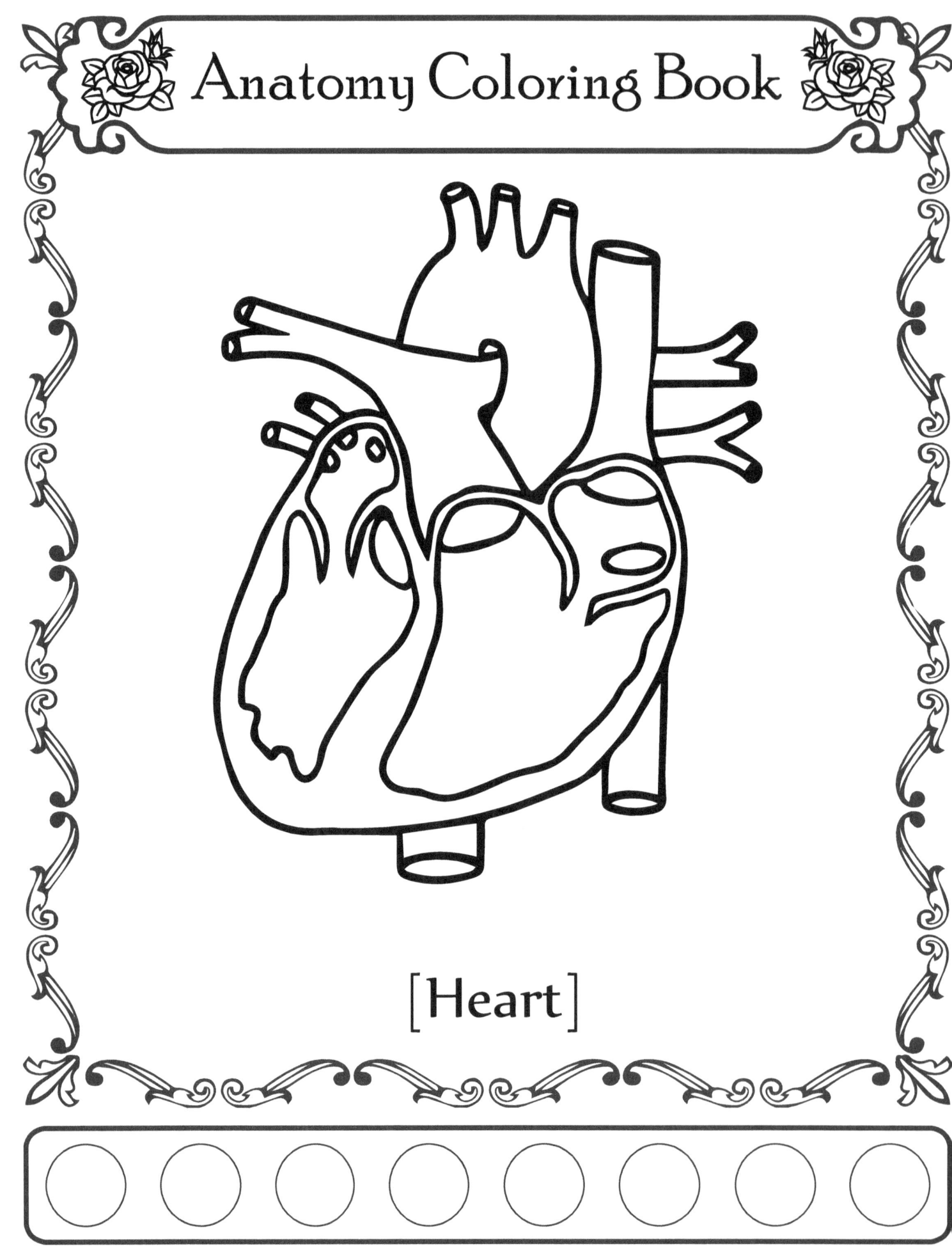

[Heart]

Anatomy Coloring Book

Anatomy Coloring Book

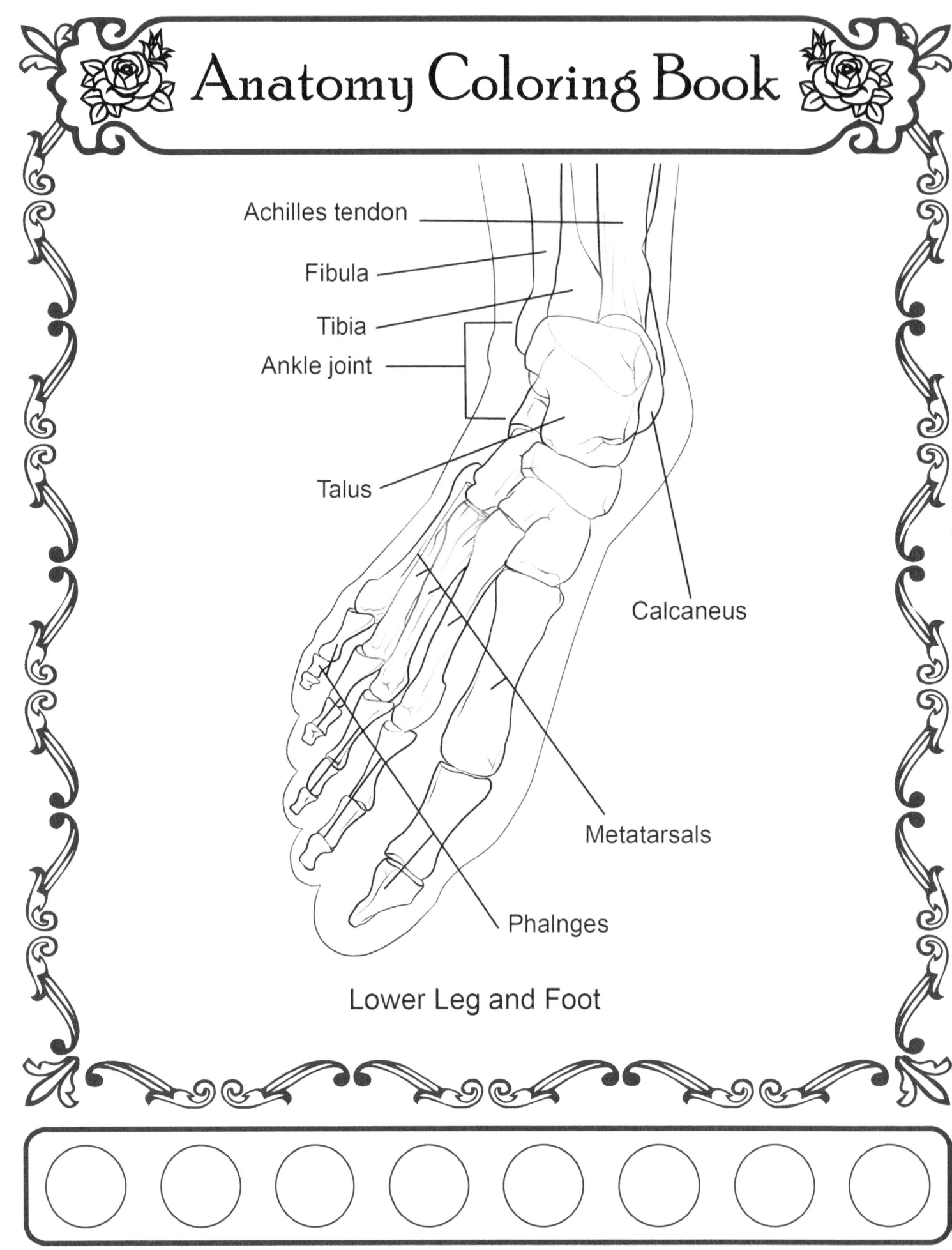

Achilles tendon

Fibula

Tibia

Ankle joint

Talus

Calcaneus

Metatarsals

Phalnges

Lower Leg and Foot

Anatomy Coloring Book

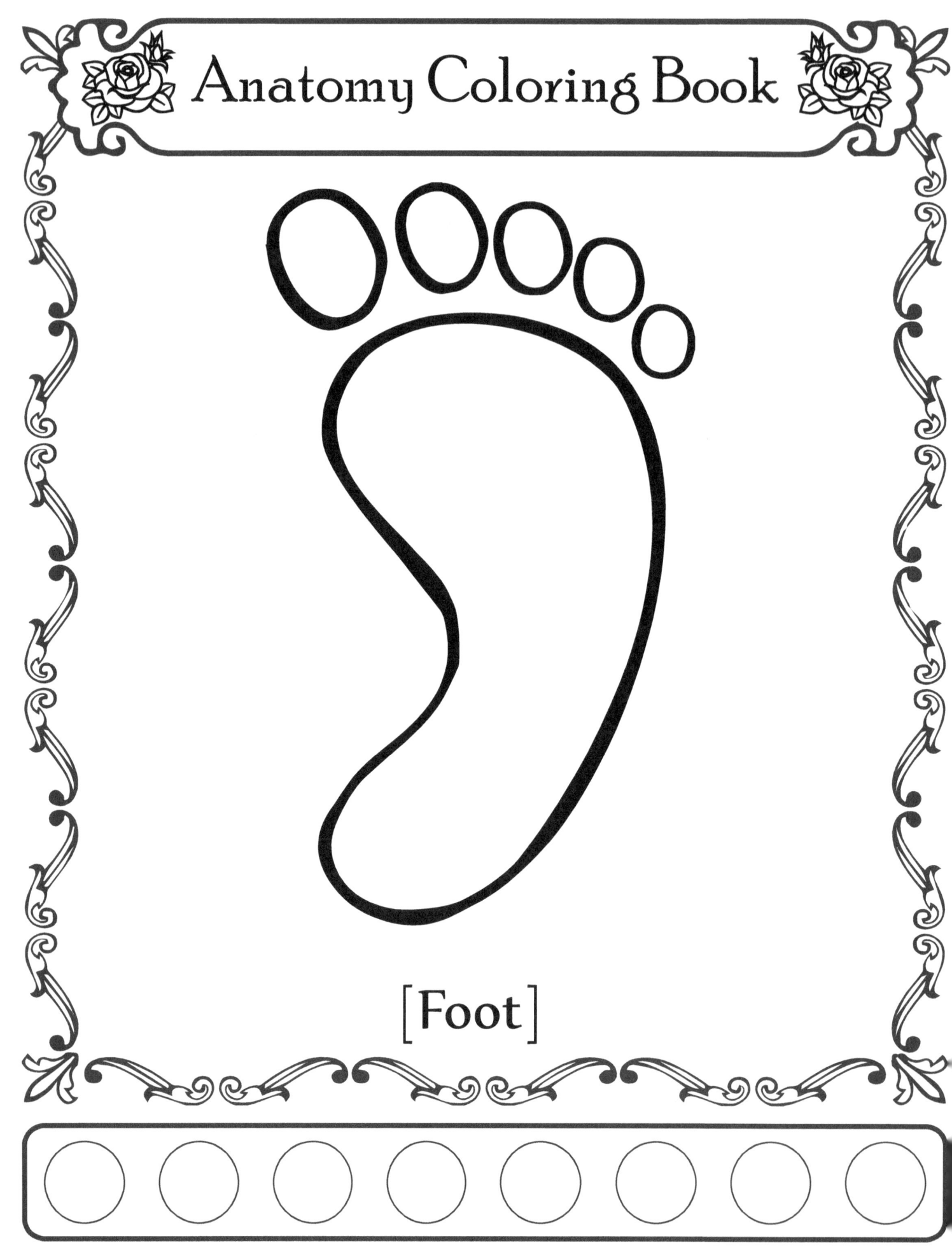

Anatomy Coloring Book

[Foot]

Anatomy Coloring Book

Anatomy Coloring Book

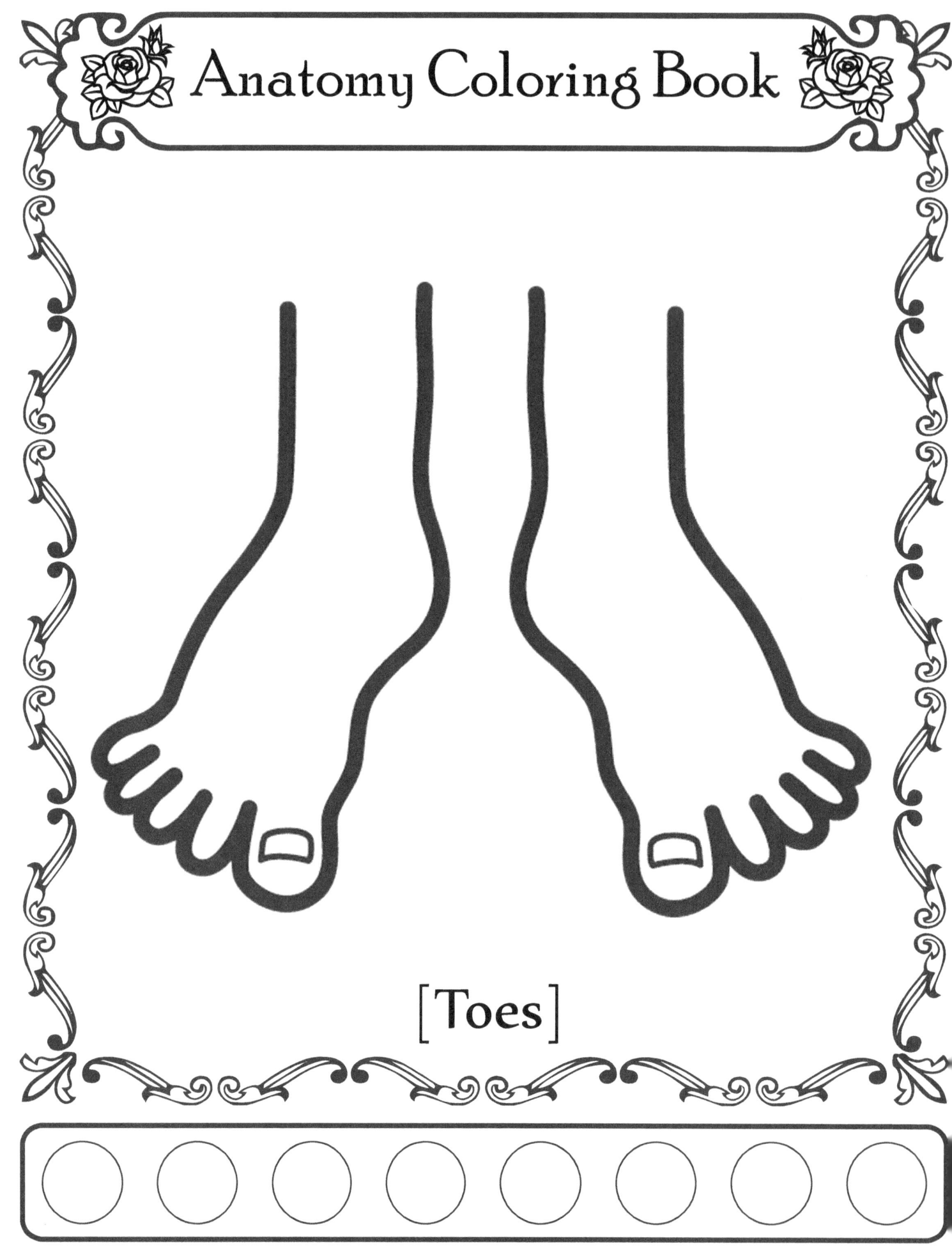

[Toes]

Anatomy Coloring Book

Anatomy Coloring Book

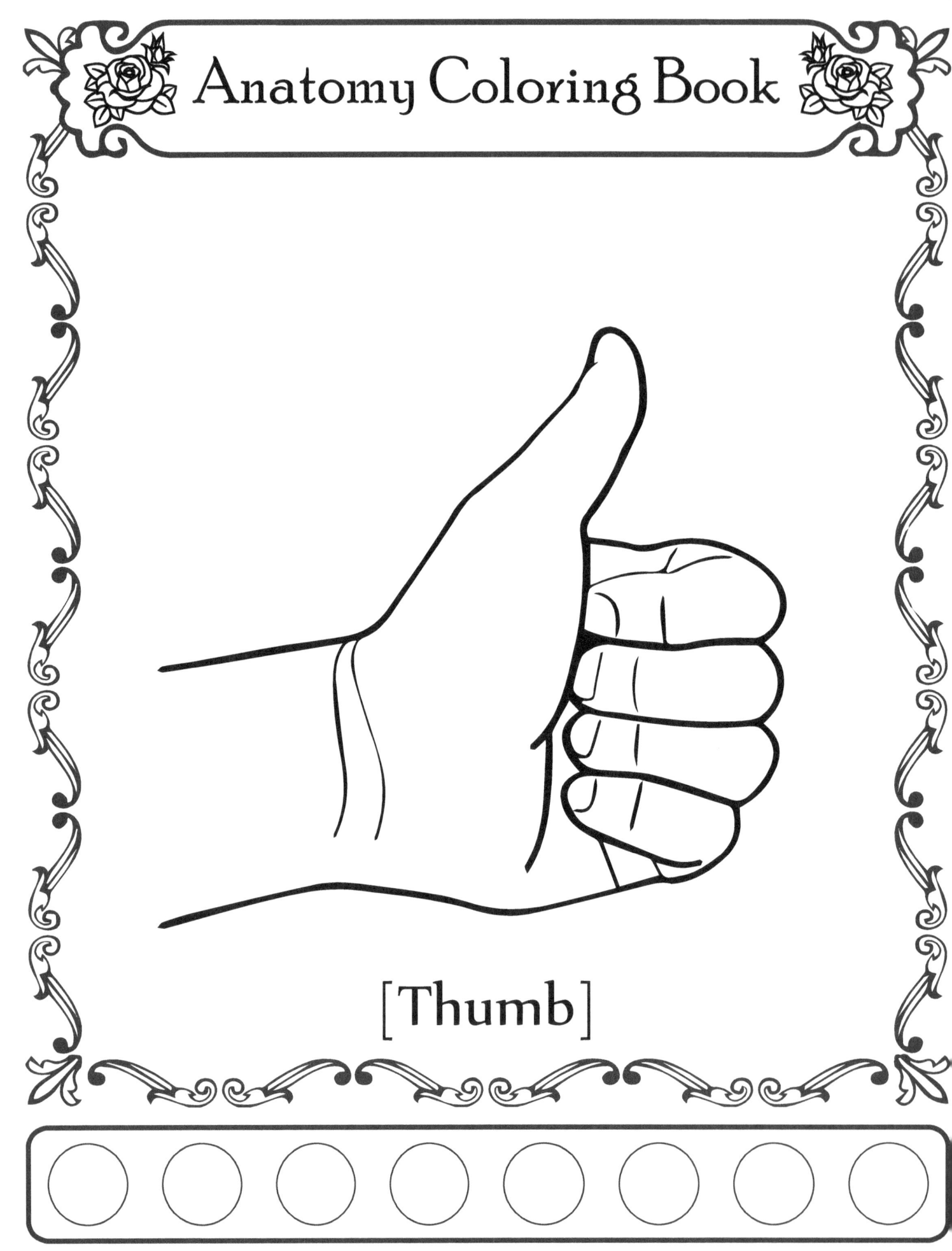

[Thumb]

Anatomy Coloring Book

Anatomy Coloring Book

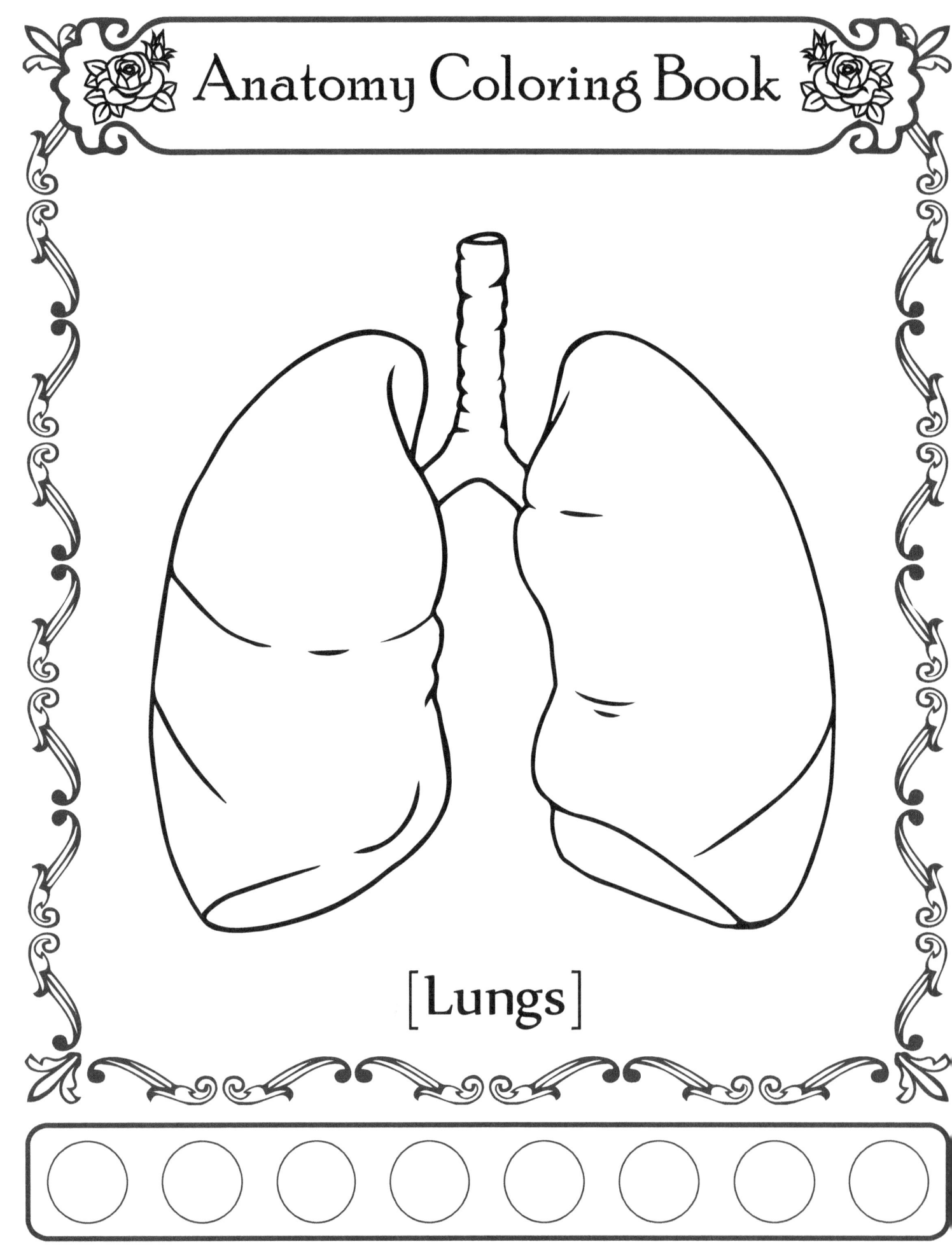

[Lungs]

Anatomy Coloring Book

Anatomy Coloring Book

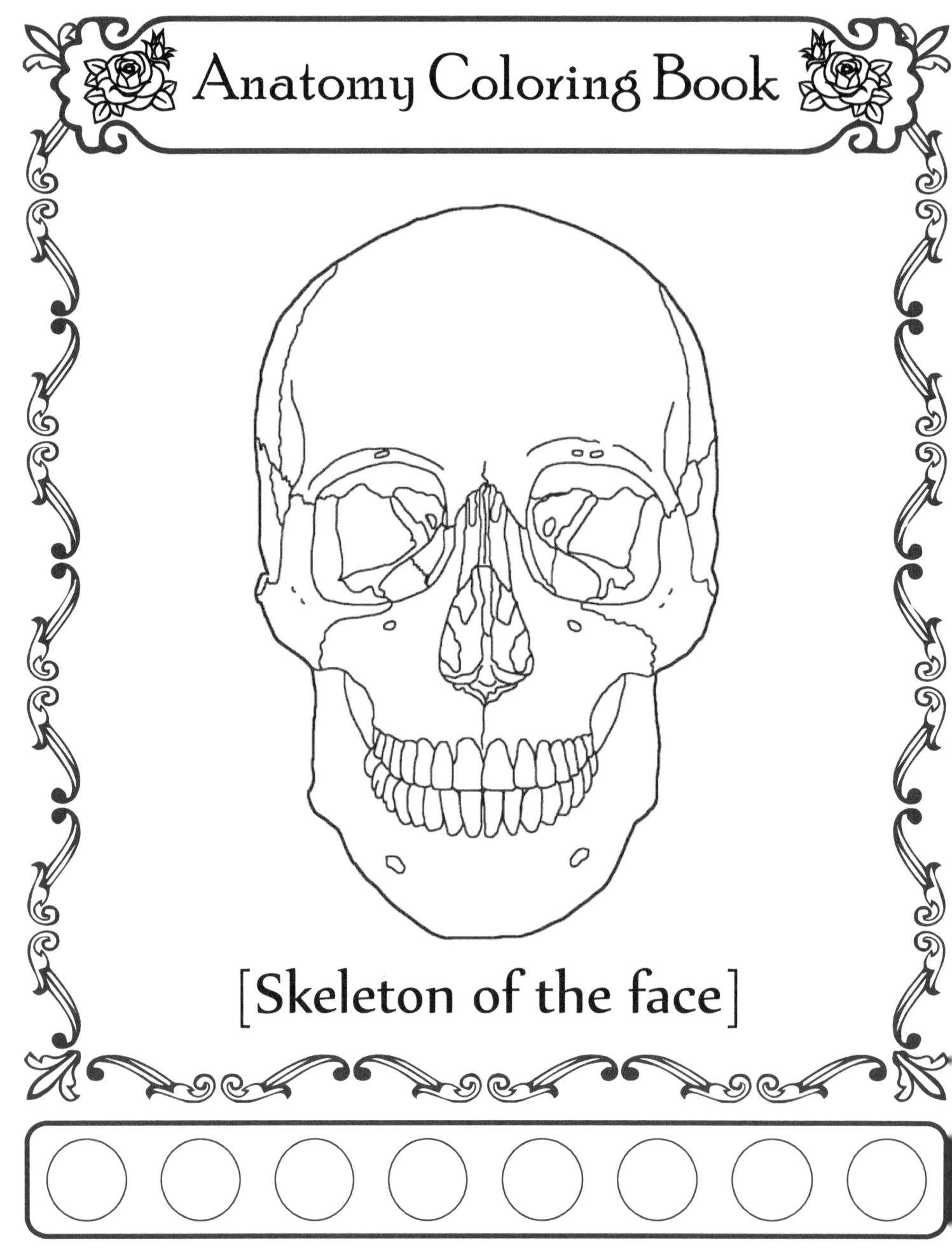

[Skeleton of the face]

Anatomy Coloring Book

Anatomy Coloring Book

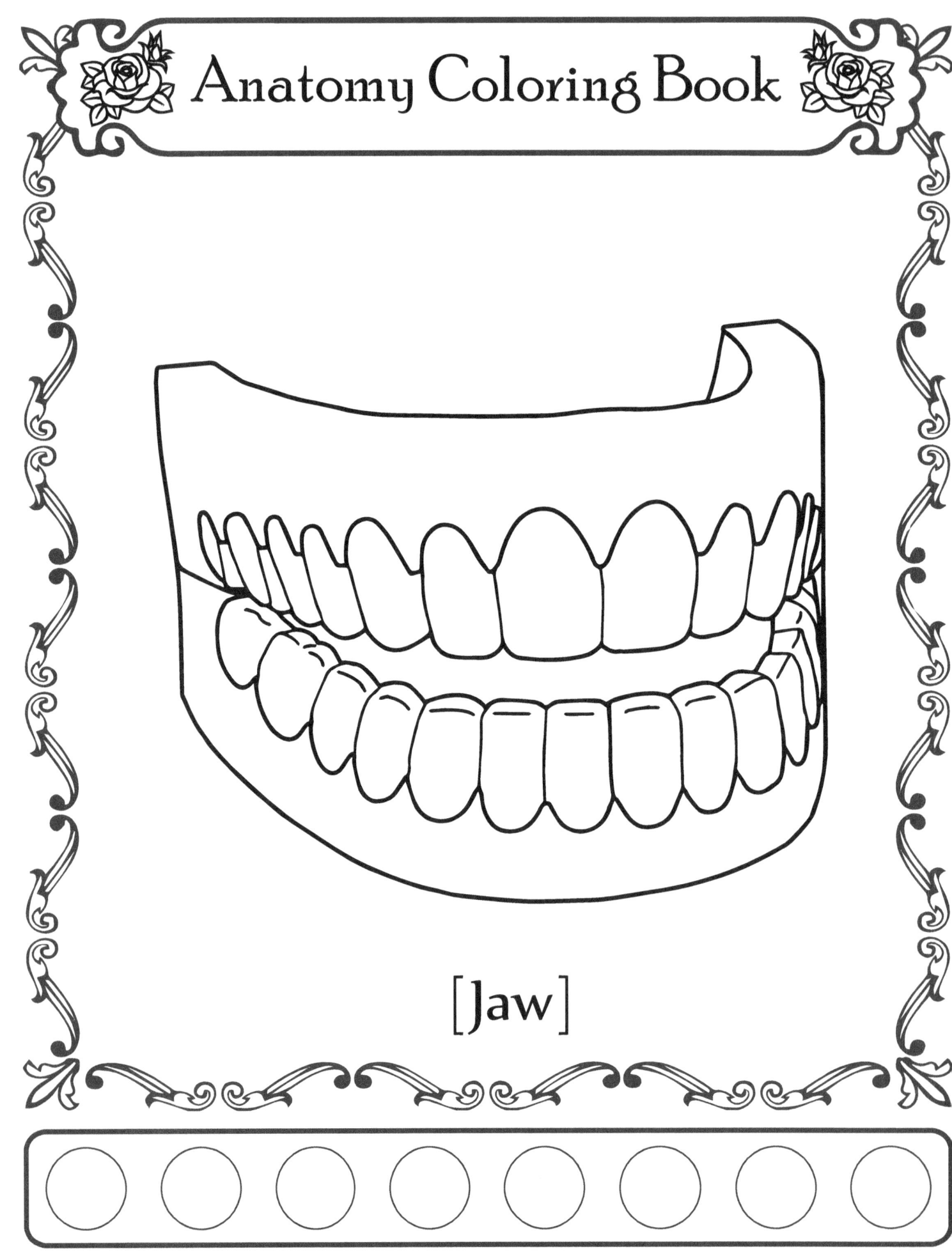

[Jaw]

Anatomy Coloring Book

Anatomy Coloring Book

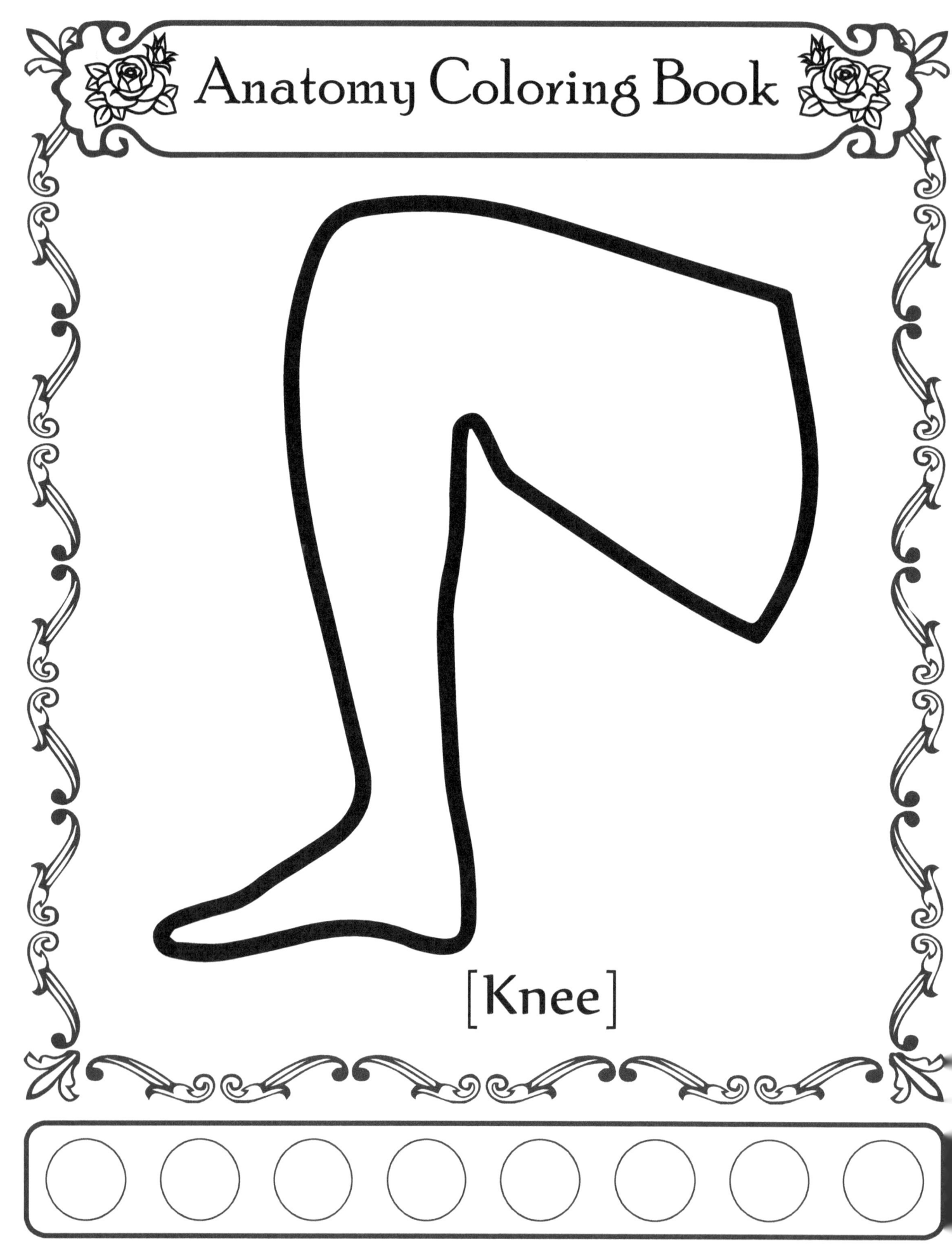

[Knee]

Anatomy Coloring Book

Anatomy Coloring Book

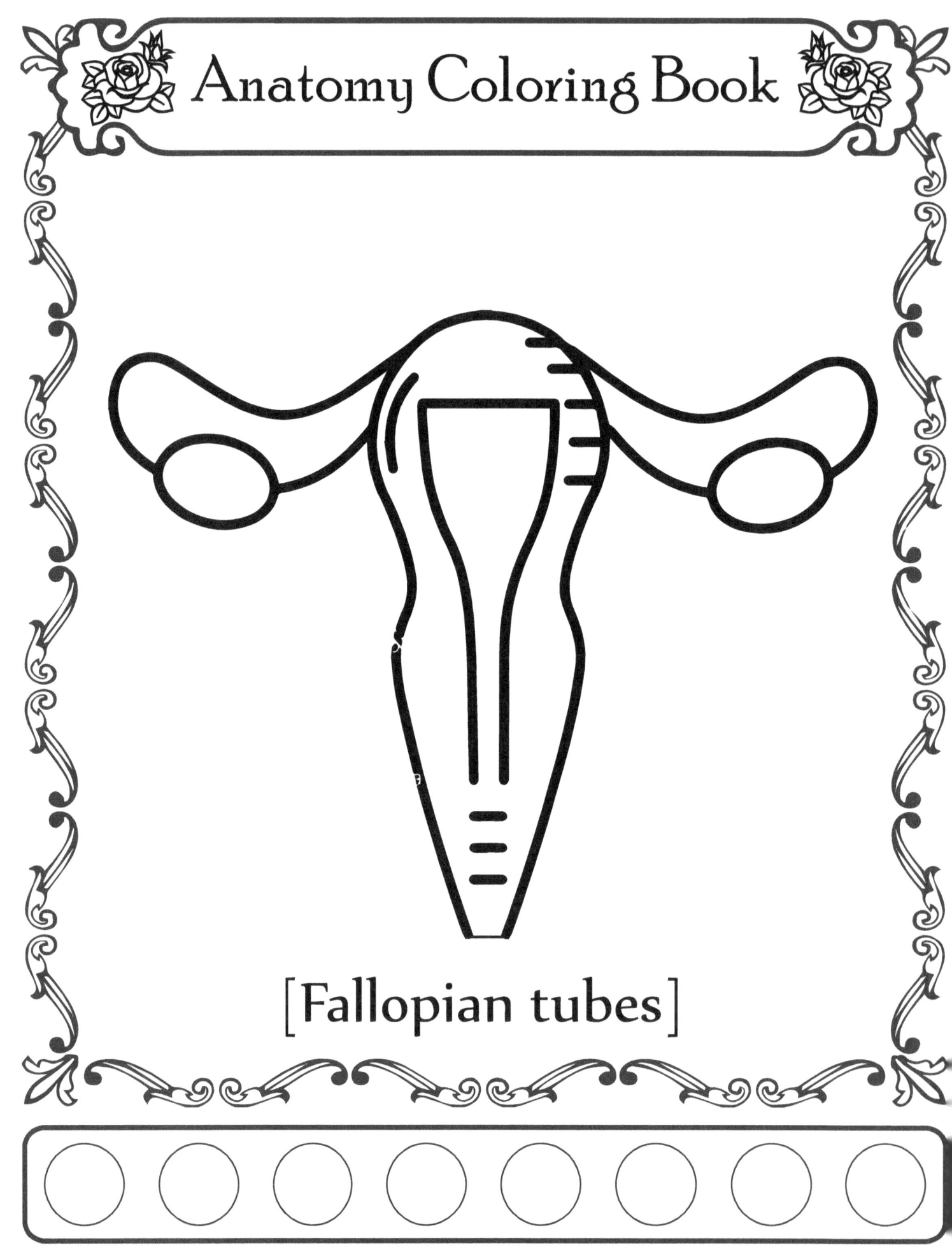

[Fallopian tubes]

Anatomy Coloring Book

Anatomy Coloring Book

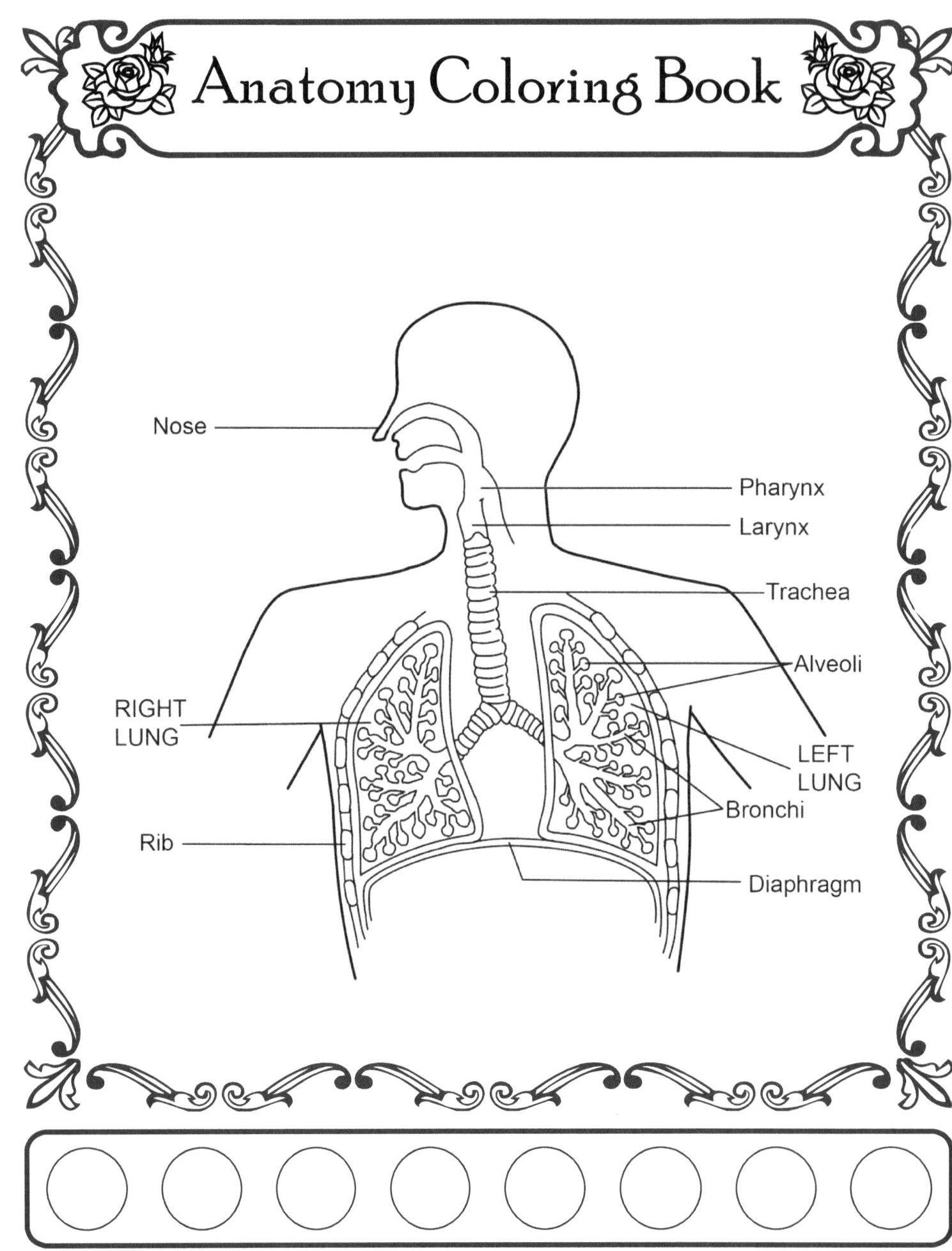

Nose

Pharynx

Larynx

Trachea

Alveoli

RIGHT LUNG

LEFT LUNG

Bronchi

Rib

Diaphragm

Anatomy Coloring Book

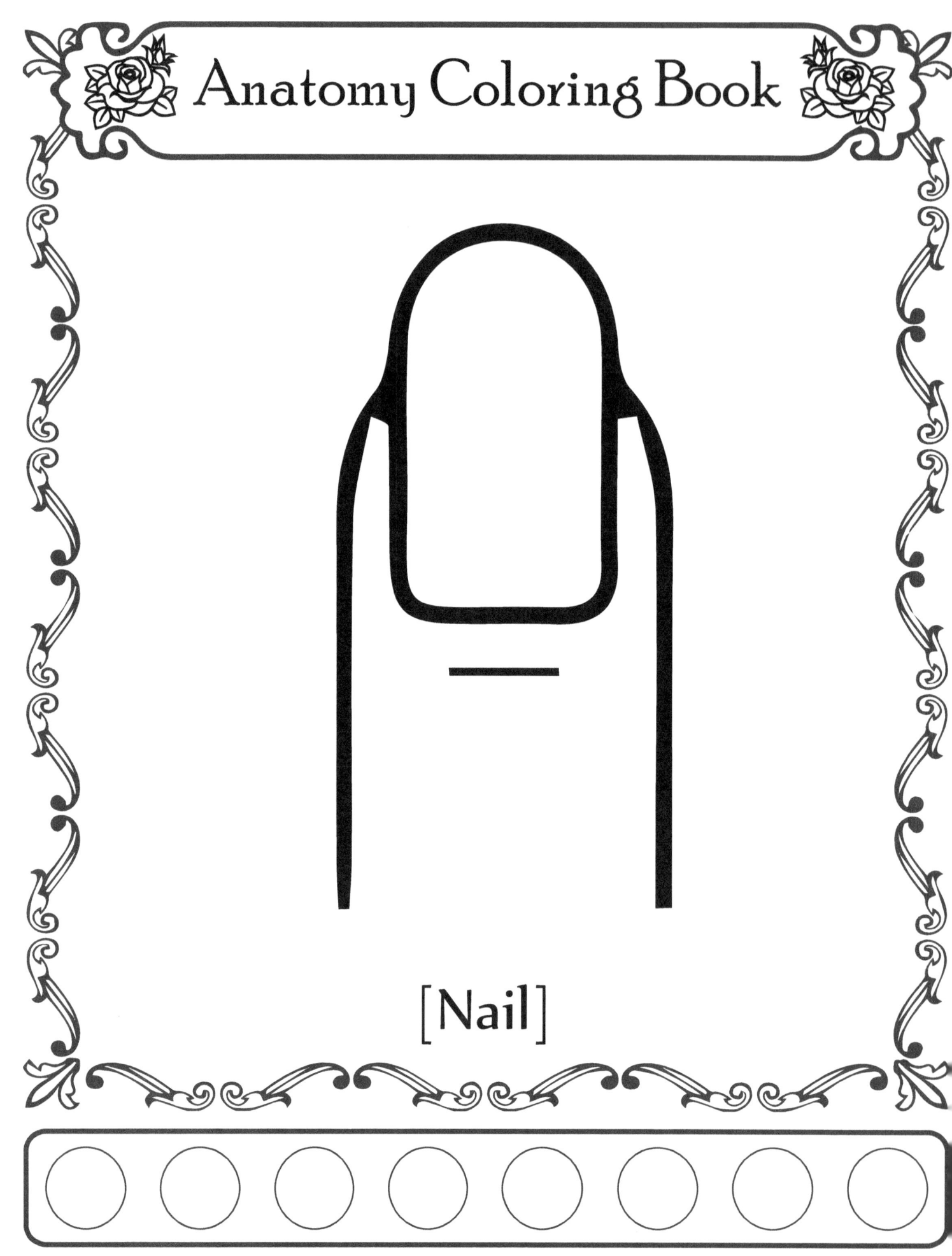

Anatomy Coloring Book

[Nail]

Anatomy Coloring Book

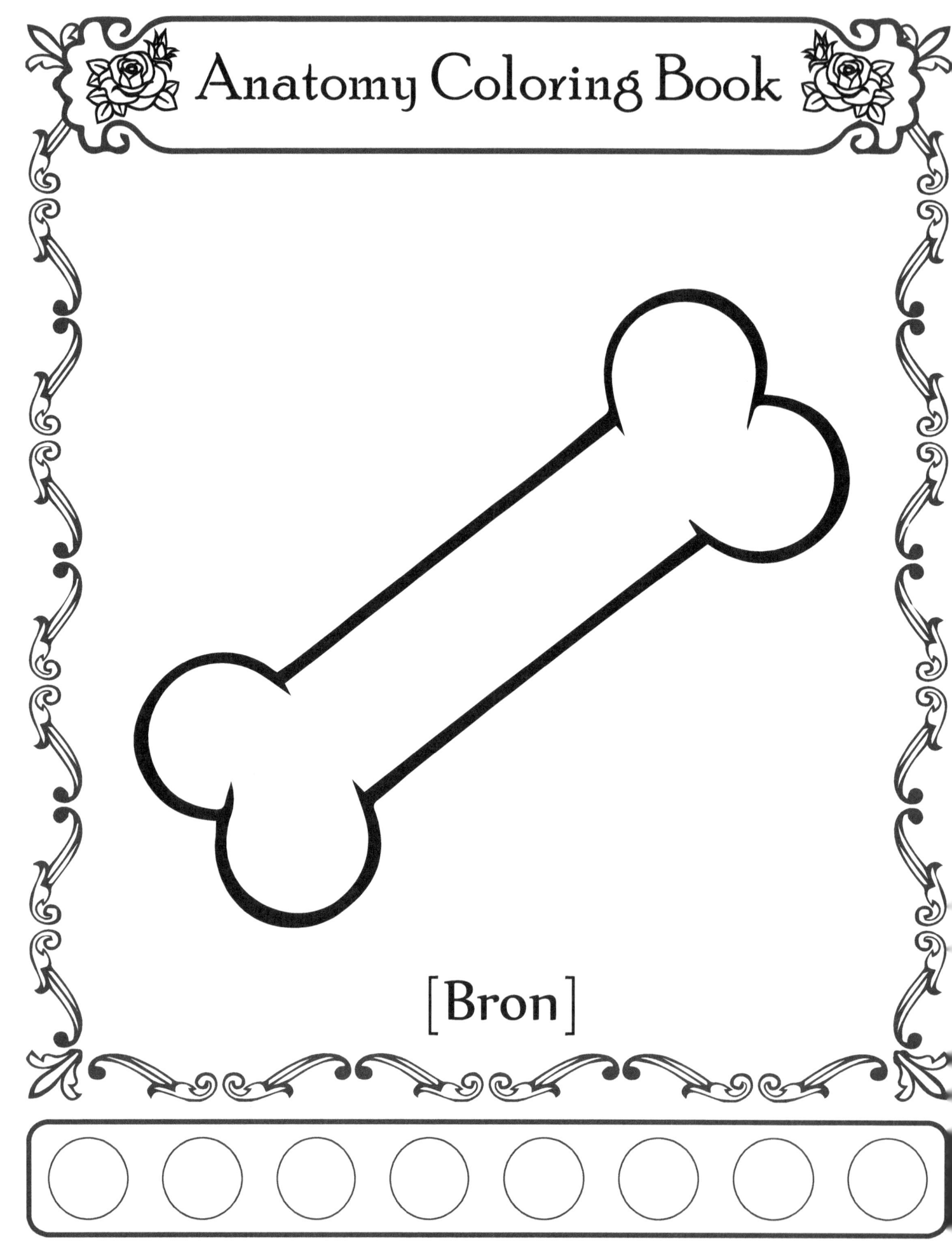

Anatomy Coloring Book

[Bron]

Anatomy Coloring Book

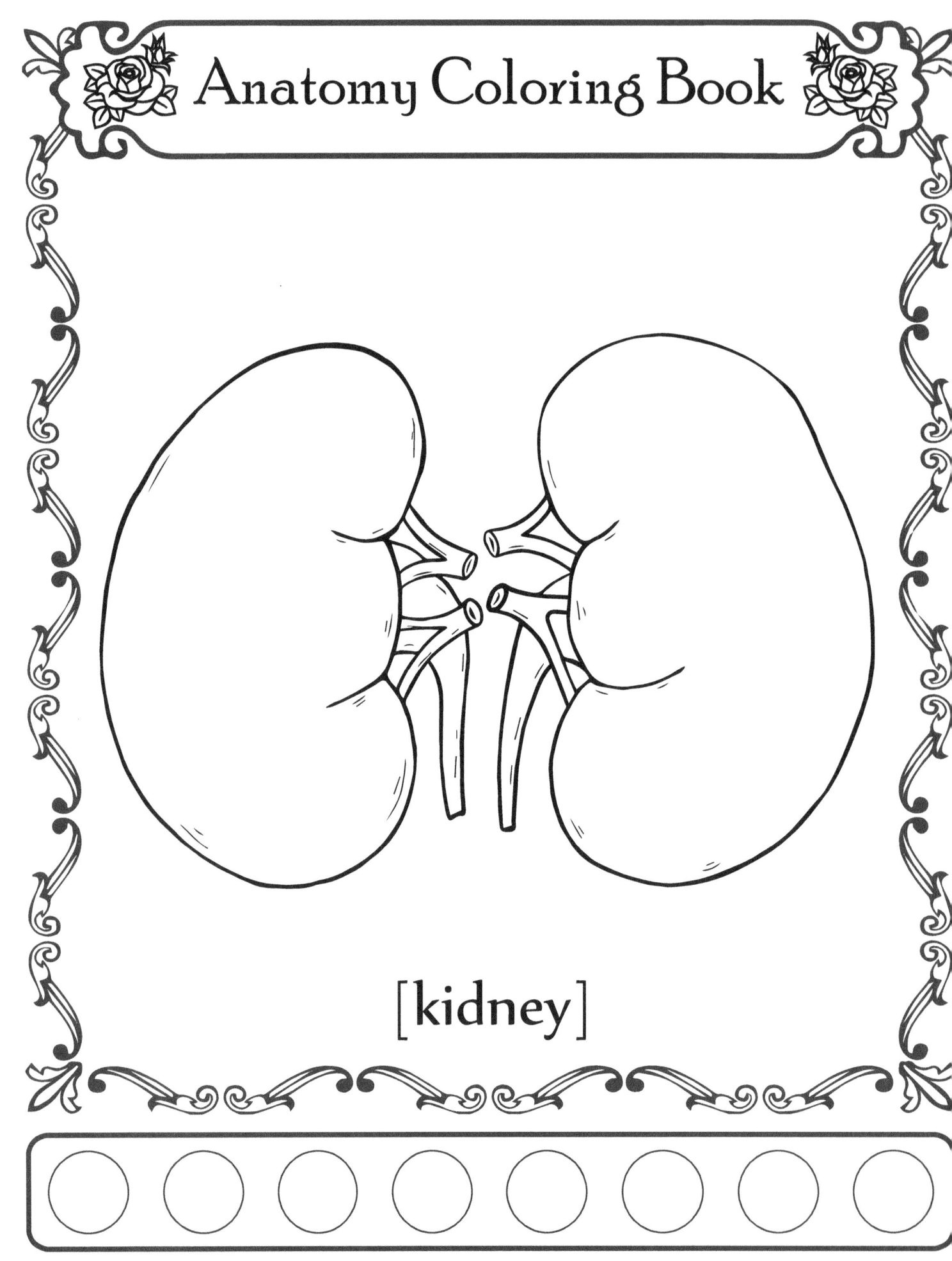

Anatomy Coloring Book

[kidney]

Anatomy Coloring Book

Anatomy Coloring Book

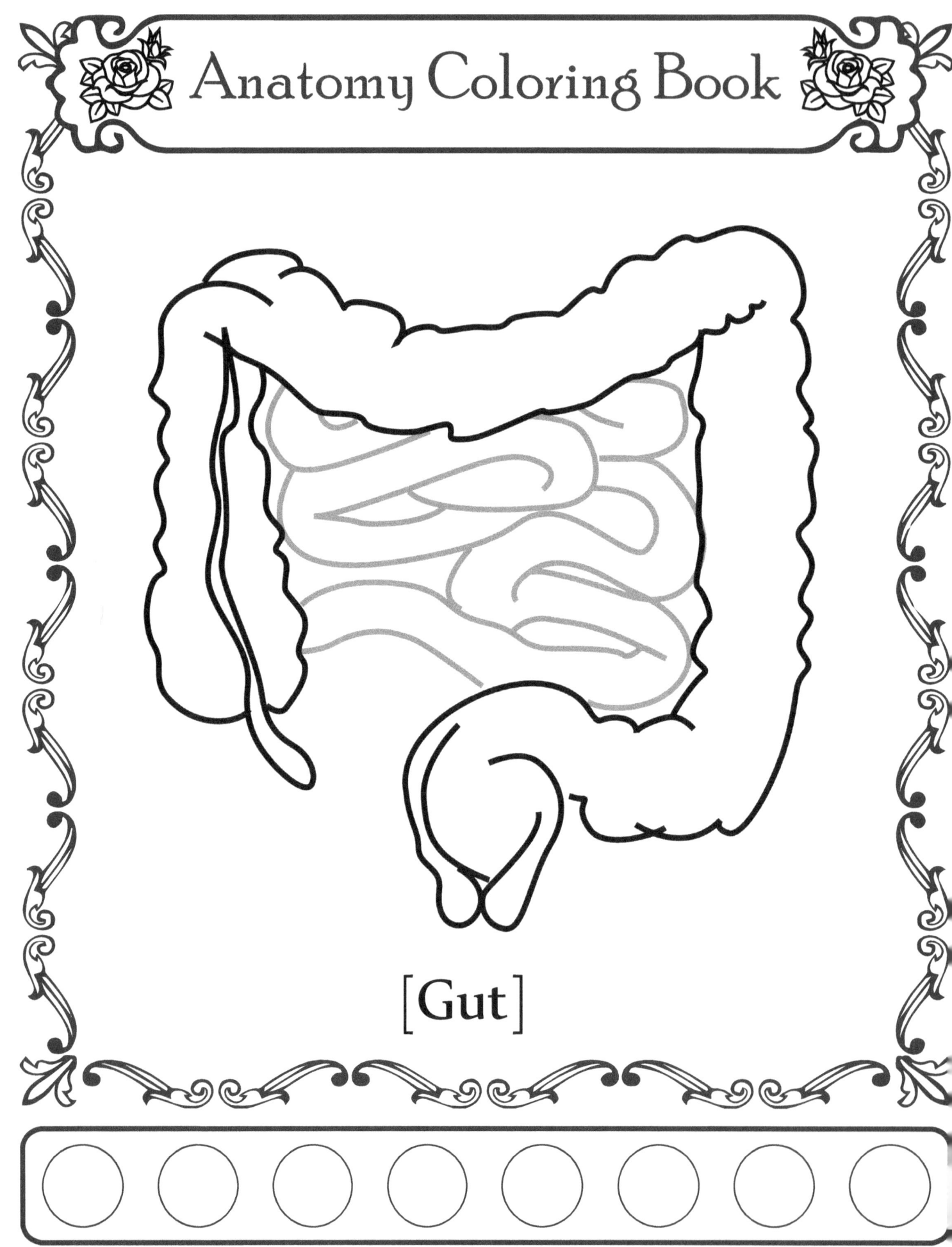

[Gut]

Anatomy Coloring Book